Ceramic Projects

Forming
Techniques

Ceramic
Projects

Ceramic
Arts
Handbook
Series

Edited by Anderson Turner

The American Ceramic Society
600 N. Cleveland Ave., Suite 210
Westerville, Ohio 43082

www.CeramicArtsDaily.org

The American Ceramic Society
600 N. Cleveland Ave., Suite 210
Westerville, OH 43082

14 13 12 11 10   5 4 3 2 1

ISBN: 978-1-57498-307-4

Publisher: Charles Spahr, President, Ceramic Publications Company, a wholly owned subsidiary of The American Ceramic Society

Art Book Program Manager: Bill Jones

Series Editor: Anderson Turner

Graphic Design and Production: Melissa Bury, Bury Design, Westerville, Ohio

Cover Images: Teapot by Frank James Fisher; (top right) earthenware bowl by Lauren Sandler; (bottom right) lotion dispensers by David Hendley

Frontispiece: "Stilted Bucket" by Jake Allee

Printed in China

Contents

Preface

It's not easy to get into the studio and begin working everyday. Sometimes it's simply impossible, and the need for distance and mental health intercede to change the normal everyday routine. Often, I start to look for ways to bring a fresh set of eyes to my studio. I find poetry brings me back to the world of making, but failing that, reading about art often helps as well. I like reading art criticism, but I also enjoy the energy of the "how-to" that magazines like *Pottery Making Illustrated* offer a unique perspective on.

One sure-fire way to get your hands moving in the studio again is to set a project for yourself. If you've had a substantial hiatus, for whatever reason, getting those muscles going again may take a little while. However, if you're reading this, you're in luck, because this book is full of several great ideas guaranteed to get your mind and hands moving. One of my personal favorites that we've included is "Molded Plates"—making multiples with a paper plate mold. This is not only a project that is great for getting your motor running again, but it's also a fantastic idea for a teacher looking for new ideas to engage their students. It also has a few unique thoughts on how to make the project special and have more depth.

Another intriguing project, "Functional Ware for the Physically Disabled," is about making functional ware with additions that make using a fork/spoon or grasping a handle easier. It's a project that hit home with me and got me thinking of family members who could use something to help them retain the joy of eating.

There are several terrific projects by Annie Chrietzberg included in this book, such as making cups with the assistance of paper templates that will definitely garner a lot of attention. This is another wonderful idea for getting going in the studio again or for engaging the creativity of your class. I can't get through one page of her description without wanting to make a cup.

What's terrific about each of these projects is that the information they contain can also inform a variety of projects from the functional to the whimsical. My goal with including each project in this book was to inspire and motivate you to get your hands dirty and your mind focused on making.

Anderson Turner

The Pancaker

by Keith Phillips

This 11½ inch high porcelain pancaker is basically a tall basket or bowl with a pedestal attached to the bottom to keep the stopper from touching the countertop. Beyond that basic requirement, the form is open for your creative touch.

Many years ago, shortly after our son was born, my mother-in-law was visiting and stayed with us through Christmas. My brother lived nearby at the time, and gave my mother-in-law a vintage pancaker from the 50's. You filled it with batter, held it over a hot skillet and depressed the plunger for a few seconds to open the plug at the bottom and let the batter flow into the skillet. The result: perfect pancakes with no mess. The pancaker she received came in the original 1950's box—everything about it was cool. I know I made pancakes every day during her visit.

A few years ago, I was pondering what handmade item I would give my brother for Christmas and decided on the perfect "re-gift"—I'd try to make my own pancaker out of clay. After a few attempts, I settled on the following design. As with any other work, I always like to make sure the design is flexible enough to make a variety of forms that will still fit the function.

My pancaker is basically a tall basket or bowl that has a pedestal attached to the bottom to keep the stopper from touching the counter. The plunger rod and nuts ideally should be made from stainless steel, however this is usually hard to come by, so a brass rod works just as well. The right-sized spring may also be hard to come by, but farm supply stores usually have a great selection. A spring from a retractable pen might work in a pinch. Finally, the #6–32 die probably has to be pur-

MATERIALS

- 3–4 pounds of clay
- 2 ft. of ⅛ in. brass or stainless steel rod
- 7/32 × 1¾ in. 020 compression spring
- 2 #6 – 32 hex nuts
- 2 #8 washers
- 5-minute epoxy
- #6 – 32 die *(available at home centers)*

1 Using 2½ to 3 lbs. of clay, throw the body of the pancaker, making it taper in slightly at the bottom.

2 Throw the pedestal separately as an open form, thrown upside down.

3 Throw a little knob off the hump so you can get under it and shape it.

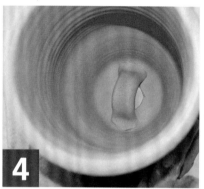

4 Attach a small flattened coil to the inside bottom of the bowl as a second guide for the plunger rod.

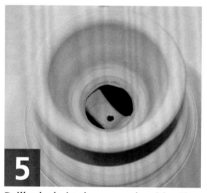

5 Drill a hole in the second guide. Flip the pancaker over and re-insert the plug to make sure the holes line up.

6 Attach a handle then drill a hole through the center when leather-hard. Check that the holes line up.

chased as part of a tap and die set. This will be used to thread the rod once you have it measured and cut to size.

Throwing the Sections

Start by throwing a tall bowl with 2½–3 lbs. of clay. The shape or style is up to you (it doesn't have to be round!). Be sure the rim is a little thicker than normal. The weight of the basket-type handle can spread the bowl during firing, and a sturdy rim helps counter that.

Though the overall shape is up to you, the bottom of the pot should be about ¼–³⁄₈ in. thick. The plug will be cut out of the bottom later and making it a little thicker makes this plug stronger. I usually taper the bottom of the form in slightly (figure 1), making a graceful transition to the pedestal foot that's attached later.

Next, throw the pedestal. This needs to be a bottomless form. It is thrown upside down, with the bottom tapered to match the diameter of the bottom of the bowl (figure 2).

7 Trim the bowl section then use a drill bit to create a hole in the exact center of the bottom of the bowl.

8 Using a needle tool held at an angle to create an inward taper, cut a 1¼ in. circle to make the plug.

9 Score the surfaces of the pedestal foot and the bowl, apply slip and join the two parts together.

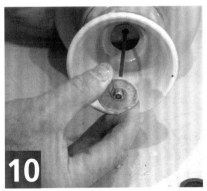

10 Slide the other end of the rod into the bottom opening, through the bottom guide and into the handle.

11 Pull the rod up and check that the plug fits securely into the opening. Set the pancaker aside.

12 After inserting a scrap piece of rod and a spring into the knob, make a mark where the spring ends.

Finally, throw a little knob. I find it easier to throw small items off the hump, since the form I'm throwing is raised up on a mound of clay rather than close to the wheelhead, I can easily get to the underside and shape it (figure 3). When you're finished, just slice it off the mound using a wire tool.

Trim the bottom of the bowl. You don't need a proper foot since it will sit on the pedestal. Before taking it off the wheel, cut out the plug from the bottom. First take a ¼ in. drill bit and drill a hole in the exact middle of the bowl (figure 4). Then take your needle tool and cut a 1¼ inch diameter circle out of the bottom. This piece becomes the plug, so take care when cutting it out to keep it intact. Hold the needle tool at an angle and not straight up and down when making this cut. This creates an inward taper on the plug, so that it can easily be pushed open, but makes a seal when closed (figure 5).

It will be impossible to make the pancaker water tight, but batter

13 Drill a ½ in. deep hole in the knob using a ¼ in. drill bit.

14 After threading the die onto the rod, unscrew it carefully to reveal the threaded end.

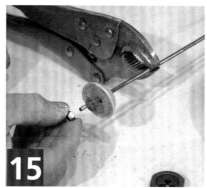

15 Slide on the fired clay plug, a protective washer, and then thread on a nut to secure the plug.

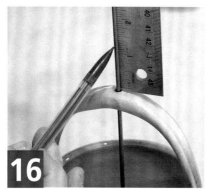

16 Moving up from the handle, mark this measurement (minus ½ in.) onto the rod in the pancaker then cut to size.

17 Disassemble. Epoxy the rod into the knob, slide on a washer below the spring, and insert into the handle.

18 Slide the rod through the second guide, flip the pancaker over and reassemble the stopper mechanism.

is thicker and won't seep out. Just make sure the plug matches the hole as closely as possible.

Joining the Parts

Now score and slip the pedestal and the bottom of the bowl, then attach the two together (figure 6).

Roll out a small coil about an inch thick then gently flatten it so it gets a little wider, while keeping it about a half-inch thick. Form it into a bridge, then slip and attach it to the inside bottom of the bowl so that it spans

the hole. This is a second guide for the plunger rod, and will help make the stopper line up and the plunger operate smoothly (figure 7).

Drill a ¼ inch hole in the second guide, being sure to drill straight, lining it up with the hole in the plug. There is little play in between these two, so be sure this hole and the plug hole are exactly in the center of the bowl (figure 8).

Roll out another coil for the handle, then pull and taper both ends like a handle for a mug. Don't pull too thin, you want it to hold its shape and not slump when fired. Make the mid-section near the top of the arch pretty thick as well, since you'll be drilling the guide hole for the rod through that section.

When the handle has stiffened enough to work with it, firmly attach it to the bowl. You want a strong attachment here as this is the area where cracks are most likely to form. If there's any place you develop cracks, it will probably be here. So dry slowly and be gentle.

When the handle has set, but before it's bone dry, drill your hole exactly in the center (figure 9). You can have more play here, and you might want to step up one size on your drill bit. You can always use a washer later if your hole is too big for your spring. Still, be very careful drilling the hole, be sure it lines up with the second guide hole in the strap of clay at the bottom. Also don't press too hard when drilling, you want the bit to "cut" the clay, not push through it.

The easiest hole to drill is in your knob. Don't go all the way through, you just need about half an inch for your rod to glue into (figure 10).

Slowly dry the pancaker and then bisque and glaze. When glazing, wax as you normally would. Fire the plug separate from the pancaker, as there's no way to secure it into the bottom. By firing it separately, you can also glaze the area that will eventually make contact with the bowl.

Creating the Mechanism

Use a die to thread the rod, so that a nut will gracefully screw on to it. Since you are using a $1/8$-inch thick rod you will want to get a #6–32 die. This makes a thread for a fine-thread #6 machine nut.

Holding the rod with pliers, carefully start twisting the die onto the rod like you would if threading a nut, being sure to keep it straight. Once it is started, just keep rotating the die and it will carve the threads. You only need to thread about a $1/4$- to $1/2$-inch section of the rod. Unscrew the die and you should have a nice threaded end (figure 11).

Slide the stopper on with the bevel side up, then add a washer and nut (figure 12). Insert the rod into the bottom of the pancaker, through the bottom guide and finally into the hole in the handle (figure 13). Pull the rod all the way up (figure 14) to seat the plug then set the pancaker aside.

The next step involves measuring the rod to figure out the final length of your stopper mechanism. Push a spring and spare length of rod into the knob and make a mark on the rod where the end of the spring comes to when it's NOT under compression (figure 15). Measure that distance, and then subtract about half an inch. This will create enough tension to keep the plug seated securely so that it covers the opening. For example, my overall measurement came to $1\frac{3}{4}$ in., so my measurement for the next step was $1\frac{1}{4}$ in.

Pull the rod all the way up so the stopper seals the bowl. Now take the measurement from the previous step and add it to the rod. Start at the very top of the handle, measure up toward the end of the rod, and mark this point. This is where you want to cut the rod (figure 16). This should be a perfect length so the stopper is firmly under pressure, sealing the pancaker, but also leaving enough room so that the knob can be pressed down about a half inch, opening the stopper and releasing the batter. Disassemble everything and cut the rod with a hacksaw. Using the die, thread the end of the rod to make a nice "grip" for the glue.

Assembling the Pancaker

Take one end of the rod and slide the spring on, daub a fair amount of five-minute epoxy onto the end and glue it into the knob. Make sure there is enough epoxy to hold everything in place when it sets. Also, make sure the rod is sticking straight out of the knob while the epoxy sets. Note: Even though it says five minutes, wait twenty before assembling your pancaker. Slide a washer against the spring and then insert the rod into the handle (figure 17).

Slide the assembly down through the second guide and then flip the pancaker over (figure 18) and re-assemble the stopper. Slide the clay plug on, then slide a washer onto the rod so it rests against the clay plug and then thread on the nut against the washer. When the assembly is finished, just heat the skillet, fill your pancaker with batter and you're ready to go.

Twisted Lotion Dispensers

by David Hendley

Three finished lotion dispensers, 7 inches in height, handbuilt using extruded parts, with added feet of unglazed dark brown clay and multicolored slip-glazes. Pump dispensers added after glaze firing.

I have been using extruders in my clay work since 1974, after I built my first extruder and made my first dies. I immediately saw the potential for making new forms through extruding, and I've always had an extruder in my studio that I use on a regular basis. Of all the pieces I make, the extruder is used for about two-thirds of them—to produce either the main form itself or an added element for a wheel-thrown vessel. Even my pulled handles start out as extrusions.

Producing work with an extruder seems like it would enable you to make dozens of items quickly, but just the opposite is often true. Be-cause of all the measuring, cutting, and joining, an extruded pot can re-quire more time to make than a similar, thrown pot, but for some forms, extruding is the most expedient way to go.

As for the dies, manufacturers offer many configurations; however, if you have more than a passing interest in using an extruder, I'd suggest making your own. Designing and making the die is part of the creative process and requires thinking from a different perspective since it's the negative space of the die that produces the form. With practice, you'll soon be able to shift your spatial thinking to where you can easily

1 Twist the extrusion as it exits the extruder.

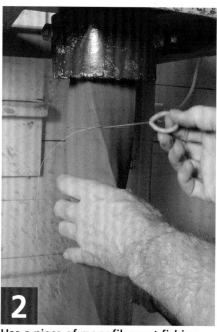

2 Use a piece of monofilament fishing line to cut the extrusion.

3 Allow extrusions to set up. Turn over after an hour.

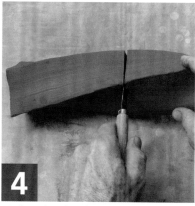

4 When leather hard, cut extrusions to length.

5 Brush on underglazes or vitreous engobes if desired.

picture the three-dimensional piece you'll get from the shape outline cut into a two-dimensional die, and vice versa. In fact, after spending a lot of time and thought designing dies, I often look at everyday objects and mentally picture what the die needed to make them might look like.

Making a Lotion Dispenser

The form for the lotion dispenser is made with a two-part die that produces a 2½ inch square tube. Hollow square tubes are among the most common shapes extruded, but twisting the extrusion gives a sense of movement to the finished pot.

Round corners and smooth edges of squares.

Cut arches into the top and bottom of the form.

Trim the bottom slab flush with the sides.

Use a tool to compress and bevel the seam.

Roll the top back and forth to compress the join.

Cut a 1-inch hole in the top for the pump.

Lotion dispenser pumps, available from most ceramic supply stores, come in a variety of styles and colors. You'll need to purchase those before you attempt this project so that you can make appropriate design and color choices. The collars need to be attached with adhesive after the glaze firing—check with your supplier for the best combination.

To make the lotion dispenser, load the die into the extruder and fill the extruder barrel with clay. To minimize air bubbles in the extrusion, shape the clay so it slides easily yet snugly down the barrel. Pull down on the lever of the extruder with one hand while twisting the clay as it exits the extruder with the other hand (figure 1). To keep a hollow form from collapsing in on itself as it is twisted, keep your hand right below the die, twisting the clay just as it exits the extruder, and move your hand back up as every inch or so of clay comes out. Any faint thumb indentations left on the clay from the twisting process will not be perceptible in the finished piece. While this process feels awkward at first, and takes some practice as well as a wide reach, I have no trouble doing the job by myself. You may want to have an assistant slowly pull the handle while you practice the first few times. It also takes some practice to get a feel for how much pressure is required to twist the clay as it comes from the extruder. Not much pressure is required, and most beginners twist too much rather than too little.

When you have a long enough extrusion, cut it loose with a piece of monofilament fishing line. Wrap the fishing line around the extrusion, and allow one end of the line to dig into the clay, which holds it in place. Use one hand to pull the other end of the line through the clay while the other hand supports the extrusion as it is cut loose (figure 2).

I always make at least 10 or 12 dispensers at a time because of the significant set-up and clean-up time when extruding through a two-part hollow die. Twisted extrusions are cut off in 18-to-20 inch long sections and set aside to firm up on a table (figure 3). In average weather, I allow the sections to dry for about an hour and then flip and allow to dry for another hour. Measure each extrusion and divide it into three 6 to 7 inch long pieces. Use a fettling knife to cut each extrusion (figure 4).

For my glazing technique, I apply slip glazes to the sections of twisted square extrusions before adding the tops and bottoms (figure 5). Allow the painted surfaces to dry for several hours before handling and continu-ing with construction. (After bisque firing, I glaze the top and insides of the dispensers.)

Once the slip glaze is dry, roll out a slab for the tops and bottoms of the dispensers. The slab should be slightly thicker than the walls of the extrusion. Cut the slab into 2½-inch squares, then round and smooth the edges and corners of each square (figure 6). Roll each square again to make it slightly thinner and wider (about 2¾ inches square). I roll past the edges to create a softer and slightly wavy edge.

Next, cut raised arches into the top end of the extruded section (figure 7). On the bottom of the pot, cut the arch so the four corners become the feet of the piece. Score and slip the bottom edges, attach the bottom slab and trim the edges flush with a cheese slicer or fettling knife (figure 8). Roll the handle of a fettling knife along the edges of the bottom at a 45° angle to reinforce the joint and bevel the bottom slab (figure 9).

Add the top slab but don't trim it, leave the overhang as a design element. Roll the top back and forth on the table to secure the join (figure 10), allow to dry for about an hour, then cover with plastic and leave overnight to equalize the moisture.

On the following day, use a piece of 1-inch tubing to make a hole in the center of the top slab for the lotion pump (figure 11). After the glaze firing, a glue-on collar and lotion pump collar will complete the pot.

Candy Dispenser

by Keith Phillips

I've always been fascinated by machines, but somehow the engineering logic always escaped me. When I started tinkering with making machines out of my pots, I knew I had to keep things simple. For one, the shrinking and warping doesn't really translate to "precision" in a studio situation. But more importantly, keeping the mechanical parts of the object simple gives more flexibility in developing the thrown form, which is what I find most interesting.

The ceramic gum ball machines I've designed employ a basic mechanism to dispense candy, gum balls, or nuts for free. They utilize a variety of thrown forms all in one piece, and getting all of them to work together visually and functionally is a creative challenge. You need a lidded pot for a hopper, a plate to hold dispensed candies, a knob and chute —both of which are shaped like a small vase. The drawing shows the various pieces you will need to throw, plus the parts needed to make the dispensing mechanism.

Making the parts

Start by throwing the hopper. This can be any sized vessel, as long as the mouth is wide enough so that you can reach inside to assemble the dispensing mechanism after firing, and the bottom is wide enough to allow for a 1½ inch hole. The hole can be cut when leather hard, or created when you compress the bottom during throwing (figure 1). Beyond these top and bottom measurements, the form of the hopper is up to you (figure 2).

The scale and proportions of the other parts are based on the size of the hopper. The chute is essentially a bottomless vase. When throwing this piece, go all the way to the wheel head when opening up and establishing the bottom diameter. Taper the chute in towards the top. The top section of the chute attaches to the hole in the bottom of the hopper

Gum ball machine #6, 14 inches in height, porcelain, shino glazes, soda-fired to cone 10.

1 Create the bottom opening in the hopper.

2 Throw and alter the hopper.

3 Create the chute from an open-bottomed vase shape.

4 Throw a flanged lid.

5 Create a small vase form for the knob.

6 An inward curve prevents candy from rolling out.

(figure 3) and must match the 1½ inch opening in the bottom of the hopper. Aside from this one requirement, the chute design is up to you. Be sure to leave the diameter wide enough so that you can fit your hand or a tool inside when the piece is leather hard, as you will need to cut out and refine the openings.

The lid is thrown upside down as if you were throwing a bowl. The gallery on the lid must match the outside diameter of the rim on the hopper, and the flange must fit inside the opening but also have a little wiggle room built in to account for shrinkage and warping (figure 4).

The knob is basically a small vase, but unlike the chute, it's open at only one end (figure 5). This too is thrown upside down. The top opening needs to be about ¾ inches wide for the 5/8 inch dowel to fit inside after the clay shrinks after firing. If the hole ends up being slightly too small after firing, you can trim or sand down the

7

Cut exit holes in the chute.

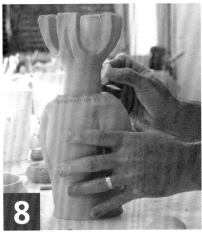

8

Attach the chute to the hopper.

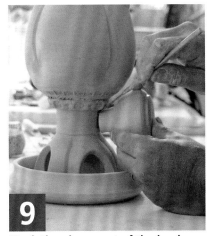

9

Mark the placement of the knob.

10

Use ¾ inch dowel and a clay coil to create the shaft opening.

11

Measure the length of dowel needed inside the knob.

12

After measuring the shaft interior, cut the dowel to size.

diameter of the dowel to get it to fit. As you throw the knob, keep in mind that it will be fired on it's flat rim, with the rounded bottom (knob side) facing up. Make sure the piece is able to balance on a kiln shelf in that orientation.

When making the catch plate, make the bottom a little thicker than a normal plate, with a slight hump in the middle so that candies will roll toward the outside. Rather than trimming a normal foot, leave the bottom flat since there's a lot of weight forcing down on the plate. I also give the rim some "tumble-home" or an inward and upward convex sloping curve. If the curve is concave or the lip of the rim is too low, the dispensed candy can shoot right off of the plate (figure 6).

Assembling the Machine

Cut exit holes in the chute when it's leather hard. Soften the cut edges with a sponge. Removing any sharp

Create the flapper.

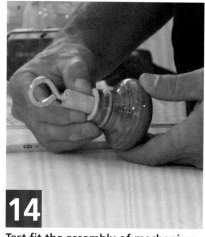

Test fit the assembly of mechanism before gluing.

Glue the dowel into the knob.

> ## TIP
>
> Make sure the dowel fits in both the shaft and the knob before allowing the gum ball machine to dry.

edges while the piece is still wet protects your hands later when you work on this part of the glaze fired gum ball machine to install the dispensing mechanism (figure 7).

Score the edge of the chute and the area of the hopper where the chute attaches using a needle tool. Coat the areas in slip (I use paper clay slip for added strength), then attach the chute to the hopper. It's easier to work on this with the piece upside down (figure 8). Score the bottom of the chute and the attachment point on the plate, apply slip and join them together.

The knob attaches to the chute after firing with dowels, but you need to mark the placement now and cut or drill a hole in the chute near the top where it connects to the hopper. After trimming the knob, mark the placement on the chute. Then drill or cut a ¾ inch hole in the chute (figure 9).

Now, use the ¾ inch dowel to help you make some measurements. This larger diameter dowel is simply a stand-in for the ⅝ inch dowel that is part of the final dispensing mechanism. The larger diameter accounts for the drying and firing shrinkage. Place the ¾ inch dowel inside the hole you just cut and wrap a thick coil of clay around it. Keeping the dowel perpendicular to the chute, compress the coil so that it's well attached to the chute (figure 10). Carefully remove the dowel. This leaves a nice shaft for the flapper mechanism.

Allow the piece to settle under plastic for a few days and then bisque when bone dry. When glazing, keep the hole for the dispensing mechanism free of glaze. If you wax the entire bottom and sponge the glaze off, you can set it directly on any flat kiln shelf. My shelves are a little bowed, so I use a spiraled coil of wadding on the bottom to ensure even weight distribution so that the pieces get a nice flat bottom after firing. This wadding spiral is also necessary if you fire your work in a soda, salt or wood kiln.

Assemble the Mechanism

After the glaze firing, you're ready to construct and install the dispensing mechanism. Use the ⅝ inch dowel to measure the depth of the hole inside of the knob. The dowel needs to touch the inside wall of the knob's top (figure 11). This ensures that when you put the hot glue and epoxy into the knob later on, there is a good contact point and a stronger bond between the knob and the dowel. Mark this depth on the dowel and write down the measurement. Next, measure the length of the shaft on the chute. You only need the measurement of length of the shaft's interior, not all the way to the back wall of the vessel (figure 12). Add the two measurements together and cut the dowel to size. Drill a ⅛ inch hole in the center of the dowel for the screw eye.

Cut two circles from the adhesive backed foam paper, about ½ inch larger in diameter than the screw eye. Stick the circles on either side of the screw eye (figure 13), pressing the adhesive sides of the foam together to get a good seal. Test fit the assembly before gluing. Here the eye bolt doesn't yet have foam flappers attached and you just test fit the pieces (figure 14). Use a combination of both hot glue and E6000 epoxy glue inside the knob. The hot glue sets faster, allowing the E6000 to cure in place. Glue the dowel into the knob first without the screw eye (figure 15).

Next, after the glue has firmly set up, slide the knob assembly into the base and, screw the screw eye/flapper into the dowel.

Materials

Clay

Hopper......	3 lb
Lid.........	½ lb
Chute.......	1 lb
Knob	¼-½ lb
Catch plate...	1-2 lb

Dowels

Dispensing mechanism template, ¾-in. dowel
Dispensing mechanism, ⅝-in. dowel
Dispensing flap, 1 in. dia. x 2 in. screw eye
Hot glue and epoxy
⅛ in. foam tape or adhesive backed foam sheets
1 bag of your favorite candy

Lid

Hopper

Chute

Screw eye

Four flaps for gum balls and small candy

One flap for big candy

Knob

Catch plate

Citrus Juicer

by Dannon Rhudy

Juicer, 6 inches in diameter, fired to cone 6 with iron red glaze.

Citrus juicers are quick and simple items to make. They're constructed like double-walled bowls, and are both easy and fun to make.

To make a finished juicer approximately 6 inches in diameter, start with about 1½ pounds of clay, or a bit more. Center the clay and flatten to approximately a 7- to 8-inch circle on a bat (figure 1). Next, open the center to the bat, making the opening 2–2½ inches wide at the bottom (figure 2). Raise the wall of the opening slightly (an inch or two) and use your needle tool to trim the inside of the opening (figure 3). Bevel the opening about 45°, leaving the trimmed part in place. (It will pop off later when the piece is removed from the bat.) Finish pulling up the center wall (figure 4) and completely close it. Leave a barely blunted point on the tip of the closed part (figure

5). The walls of this closed form will be slightly thick; but you will need this thickness later.

Move to the outside edge of the piece. Pull up the outside wall to a height of about 3 inches (figure 6). Keep the space between the inner closed portion and the outer wall flat and smooth. Using a 45° stick or metal tool, trim the outer bottom edge of the form (figure 7). Trimming the inside of the closed form and the outside of the piece while it is still on the wheel prevents having to invert the form later for trimming—a great time savings—plus, it's also much easier to trim this way.

Next, set the rim of the outer wall. I often indent this edge because it makes a great place for glazes to pool, which can give a more interesting finished surface (figure 8). However, a simple curved edge also works well. Be sure to make a good thick

Throw a 7-inch disk of clay.

Open center of clay to wheel head.

Trim inside opening with a needle tool.

Pull up wall of center opening.

Close opening completely, leaving a slightly blunted point.

Throw outside wall, leaving a flat inside bottom.

rim, no matter the shape. Thin rims chip, and items such as juicers get a lot of use and are prone to getting banged around in the kitchen. Once your rim is set, pull a nice spout, just as you might pull a spout on a pitcher (figure 9). It can be simple or elaborate. Whatever spout type you like is the one that will work on your piece, but keep in mind the end use of the juicer.

Now you need to flute the closed form in the center of your juicer. The rounded end of a small loop tool is ideal. Start at the bottom of the closed center form and pull up steadily (figure 10). Go all the way around the form, spacing the grooves evenly. When you reach the top of each groove, the loop tool will naturally end the groove. Practice a couple of times. It is not difficult.

When you have fluted the entire closed portion, pull a wire under the whole piece. Lift the bat off the wheel. Set aside to reach a soft-leather-hard stage. When the piece is stiff enough, attach any handle you like,

7 Trim outer bottom edge with a stick or metal tool.

8 Finish rim of piece with an indent or curve.

9 Form a simple or complex spout.

10 Flute center with small loop tool.

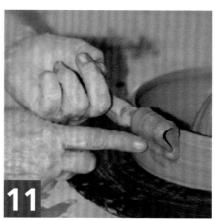

11 Attach desired handle, let dry and sand lightly if needed.

opposite the spout (figure 11). If the handle is made of thin clay, you might want to brush it with wax to keep it from drying faster than the body of the piece.

After the whole piece has dried enough to handle without distorting, remove it from the bat. Extract any bits of clay remaining on the inside bottom edge and on the outer edge. Smooth with a damp sponge. Use a plastic kitchen scrubber to remove any bits stuck to the fluted part of the piece. Do not round the edges of the fluting because those edges are what make the juicer work.

Choose glazes that break well over edges, and avoid thick glazes that might dull the edges of the fluting and the tip too much.

Keep in mind that juicers are mainly used for juicing citrus and other acidic foods. Choose stable glazes for this project, and your juicer will both work well and look good for a long time to come.

Rope-top Bucket

by David Hendley

Rope-top bucket, 8 inches in height, with ceramic and brass handle and extruded rim.

Pots with twisted coil rims and handles have been made since ancient times. Lots of beginning pottery students try making pots with twisted coils, but because of cracking during drying and/or firing, they have a high failure rate. Extruding the coils puts an end to cracking problems, as well as speeding up the job considerably.

The main body of this pottery bucket is a straightforward thrown cylinder; the extruded rim and handle that give it a unique look.

To make the bucket, use around 3½ pounds of clay to throw a 6-inch diameter cylinder that's about 7 inches high. When finished, do not cut the pot off of the bat since you'll need to return it to the wheel later to attach the rim. Once the form has set up to leather-hard, lay a twisted rope extrusion on the top edge of the pot (figure 1), starting with one end and working to the other. Use a cheese cutter or fettling knife to cut the extrusion to exact length at an angle along the twisted lines in the extrusion. This will provide more surface area to achieve a good tight joint.

Attach the rim to the pot, inside and outside by gently pushing clay down and into the bucket body, then smooth and blend the join by slowly rotating the wheel and gently "throwing" the juncture. Pinch and extend the rim at opposite sides of the bucket to form two lugs for the handle. Add decorative pellets or coils on either side of these lugs, then cut the bucket from the bat and cover it to allow the moisture level to even out. When the rim is leather hard,

19

When making the hole in the handle, push the rod in about one inch on one end, then do the same from the other end. Alternate from each end until you reach the middle.

punch two holes for the handle bail using a piece of quarter-inch tubing (figure 2).

Make a clay handle from a short piece of the same twisted extrusion by rolling it over a "handle roller" (figure 3). You can make a handle roller by gluing short pieces of wood trim (quarter round and cove molding) to a board (see inset). Just before the handle reaches leather hard, make a hole with a metal rod

through the length of it.

After firing, insert a 14-inch long brass rod and center it. (Brazing rod works well.) Bend the rod 90° at each end of the handle with your hands. Then, at $^3/_8$ inch from the end of the rod, use pliers to bend the rod outward at a 90° angle. Thread each end of the rod with a 6-32 metal cutting die. Threaded brass balls from a lamp parts supply company secure the handle to the bucket.

The same three-lobe die (shown here in four sizes) is used to make the rim and the handle. These dies were all made from small pieces of Plexiglas that are inserted in the extruder. Rope dies are easy to make—simply drill three holes, then use a jeweler's saw to connect the holes and cut away the center part of the die. While the extruded coil does not look very interesting, once twisted, it has the appearance of three coils twisted together. To achieve this look, twist the top end first, flip the coil over, twist the other end, then twist the middle. You'll need a 24-inch extrusion to fit a 6-inch pot. Lay the twisted extrusion in a circle on the bat around the base of your pot, then attach it once it has set up a bit.

Lanterns

by Debi Nelson

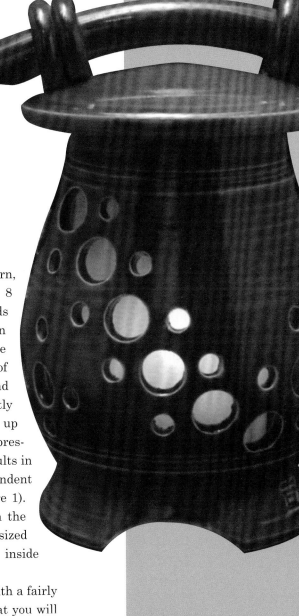

My first lantern was produced many years ago when I fired some pots in a salt kiln at a local arts college. The idea of fire and clay coexisting, both in production and post-production appealed to me. I continued to evolve the form adding style details such as accent lines and Chinese stamps on lanterns with bamboo designs. I also modified some lanterns so they could be lit electrically, as well as by candle. I've standardized the size of lanterns now so that if something happens to a lid I can remake one to fit with precision.

Forming

For a medium-sized lantern, throw a cylinder about 8 inches tall using 4 pounds of clay. Leave about ¾ of an inch at the bottom for the carved feet. Find the top of the base on the outside, and shape the lantern by gently pushing out and pulling up releasing the outward pressure as you pull. This results in a teardrop shape with an indent just above the base (figure 1). Use a chamois to smooth the edge. I make my medium-sized lanterns with a 3¾-inch inside diameter rim.

To form the lid, start with a fairly wide mound of clay so that you will have a nice wide flange to overhang the top of the lantern (figure 2). Use calipers to match the 3¾-inch lantern rim dimension. The lid is thrown upsidedown like a bowl.

When the lantern reaches the leather-hard stage, trim a deep foot. If you're using a Giffin Grip®, look straight down and make lines on the foot that line up with each grip (figure 3). If you're not using a Grip,

mark the rim off in six equal parts. Using an X-Acto knife, trim out the three feet (figure 4). At this stage, if desired, trim a couple of accent lines at the bottom and top of the lantern (visible in figure 13).

Handle

I use an extruder to make handles, but coils also can be used. Extrude a ¾-inch coil for the handle and ⅛-inch coils as decorative attachment points. Gently curve the handle coil to match the curve of the top of the lid. When the handle is leather hard, place it on the lid and use a knife to mark where it should be trimmed (figure 5). Also make a small mark on the lid and handle for where the smaller coils will be attached.

Trim the handle with a sharp knife (figure 6). To get a clean cut, you must trim the coils during the leather-hard stage because if they get too dry, they'll crumble, and if they're too wet, they'll sag. Smooth out any rough edges on the handle with a wet paintbrush.

Assembling the lid is a two-step process. Apply a small amount of slip about an inch in from each end, and wrap the small, extruded coils to "bind" it (figure 7). Score the lid and the bottom of the binding coils with a scoring tool (figure 8).

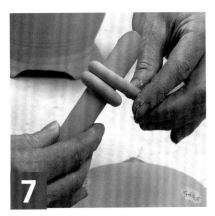

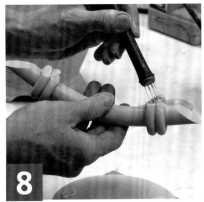

Apply a small amount of slip and attach the handle to the lid (figure 9). Use a paintbrush to reach into the tight areas to apply and smooth a small amount of slip around the attachment points for added strength (figure 10).

Holes

Create holes for the light to shine through while the lantern is leather hard, after trimming. Use a piece of copper tube about 5 inches long with a sharpened edge on one end (figure 11). I make the smaller holes with a hole maker purchased from a local ceramic supply house (figure 12).

Candles

I usually use votive candles. Even on my smallest lanterns there is at least 5 inches between the flame and the lid, and I haven't had any lids crack due to candle heat. The air gap between the handle and the lid keeps the handle cooler. Since clay bodies differ as far as heat resistance, be sure to test your design once your lantern is fired. Vent holes in the lid or a more heat resistant body may be necessary.

The completed unfired piece with lid.

Lamps and Lights

by Hal Silverman

Island In The Night, 6 inches (15 cm) in width, handbuilt, unglazed stoneware, fired to cone 5.

Island In The Night, in the light.

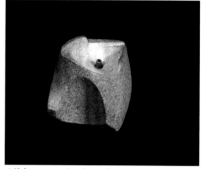

Oil lamp, 4 inches (10 cm) in height, handbuilt, unglazed stoneware, fired to cone 5.

When I was a little kid, I loved the way a jack-o'-lantern's candle lit every interior nook and cranny of the carved pumpkin, and let all the exterior become a dark frame for the light show. And when I became a grown-up kid, my first free-form, unglazed stoneware pinch pots became somewhat more sophisticated sculptured containers that held a single votive candle.

Like the jack-o'-lantern of my childhood, the matte surfaces of this kind of lamp captured the light, letting it precisely trace every concave contour it could reach, and giving me outstanding control of the yin and yang of sculptured areas. While its inside glowed warmly and romantically, its outside faded into shadows and mystery.

I called those lamps "islands in the night, because each one was a bit of brightness surrounded by the darkness of the room it occupied.

I don't think you can create such sharp contrasts between lit and unlit areas with glazed pieces. I've never seen even a truly flat matte glaze that makes it happen. (In this respect, a glazed lamp can't hold a candle to its unglazed counterpart.)

I made lots of those lamps, many variations on the original theme. And that was fine for a while. But one day I looked at those votive candles and thought, wouldn't it be neat (literally) if the lamp was simply a stoneware shape with a flame but no candle? Which is to say, I really wanted an oil lamp. Unfortunately, I'd never seen one that used its flame to help define its shape. So I mulled it over and came up with an unglazed reservoir that held lamp oil. The top was saucer-shaped with a short wick that came up in the middle (to throw

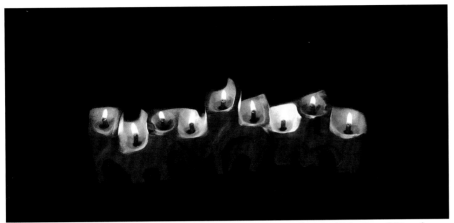

Oil-burning Hanukkah lamp, forefather of my centerpieces, 15 inches (38 cm) long, handbuilt, unglazed stoneware, fired to cone 5 oxidation.

the light). And random upsweeps around the perimeter (to catch the light). I made a bunch of those single flame oil-lamps in many shapes and sizes.

But you know what happens, you're off somewhere, at a concert maybe, or at dinner with friends when without so much as an "Excuse me," your head interrupts your concentration and whispers, "What if we joined a bunch of those single flames together? Wouldn't we have a centerpiece? How good is that?" And you grab a program, or paper napkin, and do a quick sketch so you won't forget this notion tomorrow.

Well that's just what happened to me. When it came time to decide how many lights to assemble in a centerpiece, I picked nine (my favorite number). And soon I had the making of oil-burning centerpieces down to a system. Or as much of a system as

on can have if one never turns out the same exact piece twice.

Select the Clay

First find the right clay body. It has to look good and hold oil without being glazed. To see if it vitrifies well enough to hold oil, make a little pinch pot with thin walls (no more than $\frac{1}{8}$-inch thick). After firing, fill it with oil and put it on a non-absorbent surface for 24 hours. If no oil gets through, the clay body will work.

Determine the Design

After you've picked your clay and verified its shrinkage (very important), decide how many flames you want. For the height, if you're making a centerpiece for a dinner table, you want a relatively low profile. That will allow all the seated diners to gaze down and admire the lighted top of your lamp. And it will give the oil lamp an untippable, low

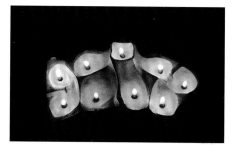

Oblong multiple flame oil-burning centerpiece, 10½ inches (26 cm) in length, handbuilt, unglazed stoneware, fired to cone 5, shown in lighted setting (left) and in a dark room (right).

center of gravity. (If ever there was a burning issue, this would be one.) So far, I've never gone higher than 4inches, after firing.

Reservoirs

Before forming your reservoirs, you'll need to know how big they should be, which is a function of how long you want the wicks to burn. One teaspoon (0.3 cubic inch) of lamp oil burns with a nice smokeless ½-inch flame for about an hour. So each moist clay reservoir has to be big enough to hold at least 4 or 5 teaspoonfuls of oil after post-firing shrinkage (about 1.5 cubic inches of oil—enough to stay lit through a 5-hour-long banquet); plus extra room for about 0.1 cubic inch of wick for a total of about 1.6 cubic inches inside volume. If your clay body shrinks 12%, for instance, you could make a moist reservoir with 1.5 inch inside diameter and 1.5 inch inside depth. After firing, you'd end up with about 1.8 cubic inches inside. You'll need that extra 0.2 cubic inch of space (maybe even more than that). Because you'll be pushing down on

the tops of each reservoir to make the cups that the flames will fill with light. And, depending on how much you push them in, you'll be taking away oil-holding capacity.

A wall thickness of about ¼ inch met my needs for working and refining the reservoir sides and top, but your needs may vary. I also found that making reservoir floors deepest where the wicks will stand allows the last of the oil to be burned out cleanly.

When you've made all your reservoirs, before you add their tops, place them in their proper positions. I sit all the components on two sheets of waxed paper on a level work surface during the entire building and subsequent drying process to lessen stresses caused by horizontal shrinkage.

Adjusting the Height

This is the time to assign the height of each reservoir if you haven't already done it. My moist reservoirs usually range from 2 to 3 inches in height, including upswept tops. To make the top of one end higher than that, weld a cylinder of the required

Circular multiple flame oil-burning centerpiece, 11 inches (28 cm) in length, hand-built, unglazed stoneware, fired to cone 5, shown in lighted setting (left) and in a dark room (right).

height to that reservoir's bottom. Instead of cylindrical reservoirs, I vary cross-sectional shapes to get more interesting lighted areas in the finished piece.

Construction

When your rough layout looks good, weld the sides of all the reservoirs together with slip, pressing their adjoining sides together firmly. If you want extra space between reservoirs, connect them with slab walls of the appropriate length. Make sure you aren't creating any closed air pockets.

Now you can roll out some ¼-inch slabs, cut them to cover the reservoir openings, and weld them in place. Add any upsweeps you want around the perimeters. And do as much preliminary smoothing and refining as your design dictates.

With a needle tool, make a small breathing hole in the top of each sealed reservoir (where its wick will eventually go). This will let trapped air come out as you gently press each top down to make the kind of concave shape you want. Ideally, this hole will be over the deepest part of the reservoir, but it should be at the lowest spot in the reservoir top. That way, if any oil should spill during the eventual filling operation, it will drain inside.

Wick Holes

Once your piece has firmed a bit, make the wick holes. I use a drill bit turned by hand to make a nice neat wick hole. The wick hole has to be big enough after firing to hold a copper tube with an outside diameter of ¼ inch, plus enough room at the sides for easy oil filling. As you can see, the time to find out how much your clay shrinks is NOT after firing when you're trying to see if the wicks will fit into their holes! My clay bodies have a maximum shrinkage of 12.5%. So for me, a ³/₈-inch drill bit is just fine.

Finishing

Finish refining the shape of top and sides and begin drying. Since this is a complex piece, usually full of thick and thin components, remember that, aside from trapping air someplace, the biggest mistake you can make is to dry it too fast. I make a plastic tent big enough to surround the piece without touching it and place it securely over the work for two to three weeks. Every day, I turn the tent inside-out so its inner walls stay relatively dry. Whenever the piece becomes leather hard, invert it carefully onto supporting foam pillows and carefully trim the underside. This is also the time to open any suspected inter-reservoir air pockets. Use a needle tool to open the air pocket from the bottom, but be careful not to pierce the reservoir wall.

Return the piece under the tent until it's well on the way to bone dry. If this drying process sounds like a pain, it is. But it's nowhere near as painful as doing all the work and the firing and then finding the hairline crack that would turn an oil lamp into a disaster. My loss rate for these lamps is under 3 percent, including the few that I bash with a hammer when some great design experiment turns out less than great. Fire nice and slow.

Making the Wicks

The wick is $^3/_{16}$-inch round fiberglass wicking twisted into a ¼-inch outside-diameter copper tube. The fiberglass never needs to be replaced. And the copper tube keeps the wick from collapsing into its reservoir and disappearing. Also, by simply raising or lowering the fiberglass above the top of the tube, you raise or lower the height of the flame without the need for any ugly hardware.

Because the depths of your reservoirs will probably vary a bit, lower a ¼-inch diameter dowel to the deepest spot in each reservoir to determine the length of its wick tube. Add about ¼-inch extra length to the tube so it will rise above the top of the wick hole. Cut the tube, file the ends smooth, twist the wicking into it, and leave about 1 inch of fiberglass dangling from the bottom to soak up the oil.

As you finish each wick, insert it in the reservoir for which it was measured (it's embarrassing to lose a short wick inside a deep reservoir). The easiest way to insert a wick without getting the dangling fibers jammed up in the opening is to twist the wick tube and lower it slowly (as though you were gently screwing the fibers into the hole).

Place your lamp on a sheet of aluminum foil, and fill its reservoirs. The easiest way to do this is with a plastic pediatric dosage dripper with a flexible bulb at the top. They hold one teaspoonful of oil, enough to burn for one hour.

Gently squirt the oil against the tubes where they enter their holes, but don't light the wicks yet. After an hour, check underneath for oil leaks from hidden hairline cracks. If your lamp passes that test, leave it on the foil the first time you light it. Now light it. Dim the room lights. To produce clean ½-inch flames, the tops of the wicks should rise above the tops of the tubes by less than the thickness of a dime to avoid high smoky flames.

Mark Issenberg's
Three Piece Vase

by Andrea Perisho

While attending a workshop at the Art League of Marco Island in Florida, I watched Mark Issenberg create his signature piece: a vase, thrown in three pieces, embellished with decorative handles and ash fired. The making of the vase is described in the following process.

Throwing the Parts

First, throw four pounds of clay into a bulbous shape about 9 inches tall with a bowl-shaped bottom (figure 1). Leave enough room to comfortably get your hand inside the pot. Measure the opening of the top (figure 2). Leave the piece attached to the bat and set aside to stiffen to soft leather hard. The piece should be dry enough to support the top section, but still soft enough to manipulate. Monitor the drying carefully (avoid areas with drafts to prevent uneven drying).

When the body section of the vase is appropriately stiff, open a 1½-pound ball of clay all the way down to the surface of the bat (figure 3), moving outward to form a solid ring. This piece will form the top of

the vase and is thrown upside down. Use a rib to scrape away any excess clay that remains on the bat inside the ring. Bring up the wall, but leave the base (which becomes the top) fairly thick to strengthen and emphasize the top rim. Use calipers to measure the top of this piece, which

Throw the main body.

Measure the opening.

Throw the top upside down.

The top should be slightly wider than the opening of the body.

Carefully move the top to the body.

Secure the top to the body.

will be turned upside down over the body of the vase. This measurement should be slightly larger than the opening in the top of the vase body previously thrown (figure 4). Cut off the piece with a braided cut-off wire, but leave on the bat (figure 5).

Place the body of the vase and its still attached bat onto the wheel head. Adjust if the piece has moved off center. Score and moisten the rim using slip. Turn the second bat, with the top section on it, upside down, and very carefully (since it

has already been cut loose from the bat) place onto the top of the body. Remove the bat from the top section. Adjust the alignment between the two sections, carefully moving the top piece as close to center as possible.

Use your fingers both inside and outside the vase and, with the wheel turning very slowly, pull the top section downward onto the rim of the body, smoothing the join between the two pieces both inside and outside the piece (figure 6). Be careful not to touch the top rim, so there is no

7 Trim the bottom to match the curve.

8 Place a slug of clay on the bottom.

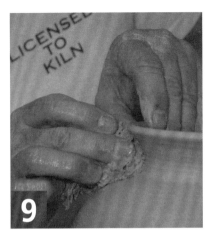

9 Throw the foot.

10 Use a drill to apply texture.

11 Apply the handles.

12 Enhance the handles with stamps.

damage to the design from the braided cutting wire. The body and top section are now joined together. Cut the piece off the bat, cover in plastic and set aside to dry to medium leather hard—generally overnight. The piece should be dry enough to be turned upside down without damaging the design on the top rim, but moist enough to trim the bottom of the vase.

Center, fasten securely, and trim the bottom of the pot to match the bowl-shaped interior (figure 7). Score

a 2–3-inch circle at the center of the bottom of the piece and wet with slip. Place a ¾-pound ball of clay onto the center of the bottom of the piece and carefully press into place (figure 8). With the wheel turning very slowly, center the clay using as little water as possible so you do not soften the pot's base. This step takes concentration, skill and practice.

After centering, open the clay in the same manner as if you are throwing a new pot. Pull up a wall and shape into the foot (figure 9).

Again, don't use a lot of water or the surface of the pot will be damaged from the excess moisture. Set aside and allow this area to become leather hard. After the foot has stiffened, turn the piece right side up.

Handles

You can now add the decorative handles. One way to do this is to roll out a 3x4-inch slab of clay. Roll a drill bit over the clay to create texture (figure 10). Then roll the clay around a pencil or small dowel rod with the texture on the outside. Slide the clay off the pencil and attach the handle to the vase by scoring and using slip (figure 11). You also can add more texture around the shoulder of the vase, using stamps and/or a sewing tracing wheel (figure 12). Clean up any unwanted marks or bits of clay with a sponge.

Wrap each vase in several layers of plastic and set aside for several days to allow the moisture content of each section to equalize. Then remove the plastic and allow the piece to dry completely.

Recipes

Marco Island Floating Blue
Cone 5–6, Oxidation

Gerstley Borate	27 %
Nepheline Syenite	48
EPK Kaolin.	5
Silica	20
	100 %

Add:

Red Iron Oxide (don't use dark red)	2 %
Cobalt Carbonate	1 %
Rutile	4 %

When this floating blue is fired in an electric kiln to cone 5 with a fast cool down (12–15 hours), a blue color is the result. Firing to cone 6 with a slow cool down (over 24 hours) yields a sage green with dark flecks.

Issenberg's Ash Glaze
Cone 10, Reduction

Wood Ash	50 %
Cedar Heights Redart Clay	50
	100 %

Issenberg's Blue Ash Glaze
Cone 10, Reduction

Wood Ash	50 %
Plastic Vitrox Clay	50
	100 %
Add: Cobalt Carbonate	2 %

Throwing Large Pots

by Michael Guassardo

Wine jug made from thrown base and added thrown coils.

David Schlapobersky and Felicity Potter are leading South African studio potters who have been working together in the tradition of high-fire, reduction stoneware and porcelain since 1973. Their open, working pottery studio is in the historic heart of Swellendam in the Overberg region of the Western Cape, South Africa.

They work in collaboration, with David taking care of preparing the clay, making pots and blending glazes, while Felicity decorates the work prior to glaze firing in one of two oil-fired kilns.

They make a wide range of items including functional and decorative stoneware and porcelain, as well as large floor jars, urns, platters, fountains, garden and indoor containers.

David has developed a process that combines throwing and adding coils to create pieces up to four or five feet in height. He demonstrates his method for making a tall vase here.

Process

Center 15 pounds of clay (figure 1). If it's too difficult to center that much at one time, try centering five pounds of it at a time, one over the other, starting at the bottom. Open up the clay to within ½ inch of the wheelhead (figure 2). To ensure the base is properly worked down and compacted, David adds a small flat piece of clay on the base, which he works in to release any trapped air and compresses by pressing down firmly (figure 3).

Next, open out the form to about 8 inches and begin to pull the clay up to form thick walls that taper inward (figure 4). This also gives you a thickish rim. Repeat the process, this

Center 15 pounds of clay.

Open clay to ½ inch above the wheelhead.

Add a slab of clay to the bottom.

Collar the clay in and keep the rim thick.

Pull up the cylinder.

Begin adding shaping outward.

time adjust the pressure and your hand position so that the cylinder has straight walls (figure 5). Pull the cylinder to the final height and flare outward to form the desired shape, about 12 inches in diameter at the top. With a kidney rib, bevel the top slightly outward to accommodate the angle of the next step, which continues the outward curve (figure 6).

You are now ready to quick dry the pot to stiffen the walls before doing any further work. First, run a wire tool under the base of the form to release it from the bat. This quick drying step creates sudden and uneven pressures that could cause the foot of

the form to crack if it is left attached to the bat. Dampen the throwing bat to prevent it from burning. Using a blow torch, and with the wheel revolving at your throwing speed, dry the pot (figure 7). First heat the outside, then the inside. After a minute or two, repeat the drying process. The clay will start to change color, and become leather hard.

After two cycles of using the blow torch, the pot should be firm enough to handle about 10 more pounds of clay. Roll out an 8 or 9 pound coil. Since your pot is about 12 inches in diameter, you'll need a 36 inch coil. Score and dampen the top of the pot

Dry the pot using a blow torch.

Score the rim then place the coil on top.

Clean up the join after shaping the contour.

Add the next coil and cut it to size.

Start to taper the form inward, using a rib to refine the profile.

Complete the shoulder and neck of the form with the last coil.

then place the coil on the rim. Cut and join the two ends together (figure 8), place the coil onto the pot, but do not fix it to the rim at this point.

Press the coil down and inward with the wheel revolving slowly, so that the outside of the coil is flush with the pot and the roll is overhanging on the inside. Now you are ready to throw again to thin out this added coil and shape the contour to make its transition with the pot seamless.

Throw by pulling the inside roll up, with the wheel spinning at a slightly slower speed than when throwing the pot. Shape and trim off any uneven clay. Once again, compress the

rim and prepare it for the next coil.

Clean the outside join and address the transition if necessary. Remove the excess clay from the inside join using a sharp trimming tool or rib, and clean out any slurry from the bottom of the pot (figure 9). Note: When you finish throwing the coil, the top flare should be a little exaggerated to allow for quick drying.

Dry the pot as before, using the blow torch (figure 7). You may need to wet the upper part of the first section prior to heating the piece, so it does not dry out too much. Clean up and remove any small dried edges on the rim.

Now add a slightly thinner coil (about 36 inches in length) made from about 5 pounds of clay (figure 10). Repeat the process of attaching and throwing the coil as before. This second coil should give you enough clay to form the widest part of the pot and start to curve the form back in, finishing up to the shoulder of the pot (figure 11). Clean up and dry the pot as before. Note that the bevel at the top edge should slope gently inwards for the final coil, which will become the rim of the pot.

Add a final coil, rolled out from about 2 to 3 pounds of clay. Throw the desired neck and rim (figure 12) and clean up the inside of the pot and the transition as before. The final coil allows for a bit of creativity. You can finish off these tall forms as vases, jars, or bottles. Dry as before and add accents like lugs, handles and or sprigs. Your final pot will be around 28 to 30 inches tall.

Glazing

David and Felicity usually skip the bisque fire, but their glazing technique is the same for greenware or bisqueware. After spraying the entire pot with a glaze, they add brushwork decoration using various oxides and pigments. After thoroughly drying the pots, the work is fired to cone 12 in a gas kiln in a reducing atmosphere.

One Piece Goblets

by Jan Parzybok

Green Mountain Goblet, Orchid Cordial and Blue Rim Goblets, clear glaze, Mason stain decoration, fired to cone 6.

As with any functional pot you throw, it's important to study and understand the geometry and physics of the pot to make it do what it's designed to do and still be beautiful. A clay goblet is a specialty item that must be well balanced and perfectly functional. Goblets made from separate thrown parts often end up looking like two pieces stuck together. Throwing a solid stem goblet from one piece of clay results in a more integrated piece with a good heft in the hand. The solid stem creates a weighted bottom for balance and allows for a long, lean line with visually appealing elegance.

Creating the Cup

Center two pounds of clay into a 5-inch tall mound on the wheel. Keep in mind the bottom of the leather hard goblet will be trimmed to 3¼ inches wide, so leave a little extra clay at the base while throwing.

Slow the wheel. Open the mound of clay down to about two inches in the very center of the clay. It's important not to make the cup too large for the stem, as the goblet may become top heavy when filled with wine. Also, making a large cup will not leave enough clay for the stem, and an overly thin stem may warp in the kiln because it cannot support the cup's weight. As a general rule, for balanced proportions and aesthetics, the cup should be roughly 3 inches of the total 7½ inch finished height.

Define the inside and outside bottom of the cup shape (figure 1). Firmly compress the inside bottom of the cup with a finger to align clay particles and avoid "S" cracks. Next, pull the side of the cup to its finished shape. Flare the lip slightly to the final 3¼ inches. Be careful not to flare the rim too wide. As with a mug lip, a radical flare allows too much liquid

After opening the clay, define the inside and outside of the cup shape.

The diameter and height of the cup should be roughly equal.

Move the clay slowly up from the bat with equal pressure from both hands.

Using a wire tool and water, slide the goblet off of the bat.

Begin trimming using a wide tool to flatten the bottom of the foot.

Trim to the scribed line for the outside foot diameter with a ribbon loop tool.

to flow out of the cup at one time.

Use calipers to check that both the diameter and height are approximately 3¼ inches (figure 2). Finish the lip with a chamois and the cup is complete. You won't be able to return to make any changes on it, so if you see imperfections, you'll need to address them before continuing.

Throwing the Stem

Any throwing sponge works well for this, and I use a thin folded sponge from a box of small Orton cones. The sponge maintains a consistently lubricated surface on the clay. Slow

the wheel again. As in throwing other forms (almost like collaring in the neck of a bottle), apply equal pressure to both sides of the clay stem, which will force the clay up (figure 3). The piece is top heavy, so use caution and allow the stem to remain a bit thicker than you want the finished piece to be. You can trim away some of the excess later. Two to three efficient pulls should be enough; overworked clay will be prone to cracking. Keep the cup on center as much as possible until the lip touches the wire guide. This is a

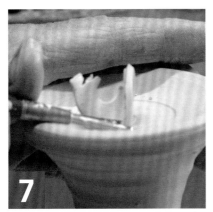

7 Leave ¼ inch for the foot ring, and trim to ½ inch deep at the center.

8 Compress the base of the stem to prevent "S" cracks.

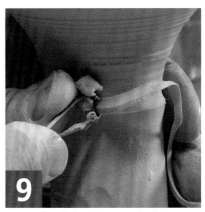

9 Brace the ribbon tool and trim the stem downwards towards the cup.

10 Continue to taper the stem through gradual trimming.

11 Finalize the stem design, smooth and finish the surface with your fingers.

**Blue Mountain Goblet,
7½ inches in height,
sgraffito, fired to cone 6.**

trouble spot because the cup is top heavy. Be patient with yourself.

Undercut with your wire and water to slide the goblet off the bat or gently lift it off by the stem (figure 4). Don't be too concerned if the cup is not perfectly on center. After it has dried for two to three hours, return the goblet to center on the wheel, and straighten it if it's not vertical. At this stage a good deal of manipulating never brings the cup to true center. When they are leather hard, and ready for trimming, you can perfect them.

Wrap the cups lightly in plastic, leaving the stems uncovered to air-dry overnight. More or less time may be necessary depending on the temperature and humidity level in your studio. The stems must be sturdy, on the hard side of leather (only a small dimple occurs when you press hard on the clay), when trimming begins.

Trimming

Attach the goblet securely to the wheel head using four lugs of clay or use a Giffin Grip. Before you start to trim, adjust the stem to ensure it's as perpendicular to the wheel as possible. Now, use a wide trimming tool to flatten the bottom. The goblet base should be perfectly parallel with the wheel head.

Measure and scribe the outside foot diameter with your calipers (figure 5). Using a ribbon tool, trim it to 3¼ inches (figure 6). Move in ¼ inch towards the center to define the inside of the foot diameter. Begin trimming from this line towards the center. Trim to a depth of ½ inch (figure 7). This creates a visually appealing foot and ensures that at least one full tablespoon of water spills as the goblet is delivered from dishwasher to cupboard.

Carefully compress the base of the stem to ensure no "S" cracks appear later (figure 8). You won't have another opportunity to compress this portion of the stem, as the untrimmed thickness of the stem can support the pressure, but the trimmed stem won't be able to. Complete all work (including making your potter's mark) on the foot before trimming the stem.

Allow the stem of the carefully se-

cured goblet to slip freely through your fingers. Concentrate on holding the ribbon tool still with your right hand and bracing it with your left thumb (figure 9). Begin trimming ¼ inch under the foot and move downward. In the first course of trimming, aim just to peel off any asymmetrical clay from the entire stem. This makes the stem smooth, symmetrical and perpendicular—much easier on which to work.

Begin designing at the foot first while the stem is still relatively thick and can withstand some pressure. Keep in mind that the more clay you remove, the more vulnerable the stem becomes. The more clay you leave, the clunkier it looks. Occasionally study the piece right side up as you work.

Taper the stem from foot to cup in a bold sweeping gesture (figure 10). To make sure the stem remains sturdy, trim no more than a ¾ inch diameter at the narrowest point. Finalize the stem design and finish the surface with your finger or moist sponge (figure 11).

Tips & Troubleshooting

- Cup moves off center: Moving too much clay up at once, or the wheel is spinning too fast.

- Lopsided stem: Uneven pressure from each hand as you move the clay.

- A "V" develops inside of the cup: you're distorting and moving the cup rather than the stem.

- If you're making a set of goblets, cut a cardboard template (cereal boxes work well) after your first trimmed goblet to design the others.

- When bisque firing the goblets, allow them to heat slowly during the first 212° Fahrenheit. Do not stack them.

- Solid stem goblets lend themselves to carving and texturing.

- When glazing goblets, hold them by the stem.

- Test your finished goblets to see if they tip easily. Your goal is to make them elegant as well as truly functional, so if your first design is too unstable, modify or revise it and make some more!

- When I throw a set of goblets, each stem has a different design. That way, after the third glass, a wine drinker can recognize his or her own goblet.

Textured Cups

by Annie Chrietzberg

PHOTOS OF FINISHED PIECES BY ADAM HOLLOWAY

Form, function and surface all work together to make cups the ideal utilitarian object to show off your talents. This collection of slab-built textured cups embodies an exploration of these qualities.

Cups, cups, cups. Sometimes they are the first pieces an aspiring potter attempts. Often they are the first part of a potter's repertoire to come into focus. Cups are a good way to get back into a making cycle after a hiatus, and a good warm up for a day of making once on a roll.

Cups are the calling cards we trade with other potters, the tokens of our long days in the studio that we give to our loved ones. I recently attended a slide lecture given by the potter Josh Deweese and something he said stuck with me: "Cups are the potter's most successful form because they are so accessible, and therefore have the ability to truly live in people's lives on a day to day basis. The relationship that develops with a cup is quite intimate, and is a great way to bring art into people's lives."

Cups are taken to work, carried out into the yard, whisked off for rides in the car. Once broken, a great cup lingers in the memory as "one that got away." The really good mugs migrate to the front of the cupboard, while the mugs with less balance and grace end up dusty, shoved to the back corner.

Cups are small and quickly made in relation to other forms. They're a great venue for trying new ideas and sorting through forms and textures. Right now I choose to make each cup

"Two Dotted Cups." Cups are small and quickly made in relation to other forms, and are a great venue for trying new ideas and sorting through form and texture.

by hand, reinterpreting the shape of a favorite thrown form with my textured slab cups. I aspire to the perfect radial symmetry that the Yixing potters achieve, though I must admit I'm not quite there. Even so, my cups are exquisite in their almost-perfection, and my customers really appreciate the details and the focus evident in each one.

Process

In this technique, which evolved after attending a Sandi Pierantozzi workshop, start by making a trun-

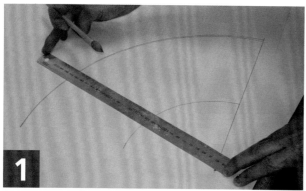

1 A cup pattern begins with a template for a truncated cone. The top arc is the diameter of the rim and the bottom arc is the diameter of the base.

2 Create an assortment of templates. Keep notes on them as you use them.

3 Roll out a slab and cut the clay leaving ¼ to ½ inch around the template.

4 Place the slab on a textured surface and gently roll it into the texture. Dust the texture with cornstarch for easy release.

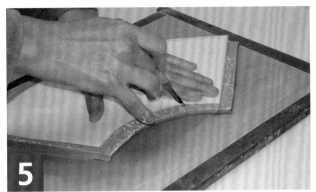

5 Place the template back on the slab and cut around it angling the knife 45° on the sides but cutting the top and bottom perpendicular.

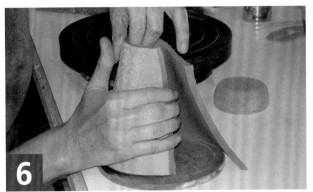

6 Set the piece on a small bat with the lip on the bottom, and use the joining edge to bend the piece around. Handle carefully to preserve the texture.

7 Score and slip both of the edges and press the seam together across the beveled cut, using a light but firm touch.

8 Use a tool instead of your finger on the inside applying just enough pressure that you can feel the tool moving across the inside.

cated cone template with a heavier-weight paper. Once assembled, the cone can be left with a hard line, or manipulated from the inside or outside to create or reduce the volume. If you have a particular size of cup in mind, start by approximating measurements with a measuring tape, remembering to account for the shrinkage of your clay body.

Draw a truncated cone from two arcs of concentric circles. Use the same central point not only to draw the arcs, but also to create the sides of the template, which become the seam of the cup. Keep notes about

what you're making on your templates, like which handle template you use with a particular cup template. I have some templates that I use for multiple forms, and so I list the form and its related templates.

Use clay that is well-aged and nice and plastic, but not too wet, allowing you to handle intricate texture without marring it. Roll out a nice even slab, infuse it with a luscious texture, then cut out the cone, using your template. To increase the joining surface, angle the knife tip on the sides of the template, which is to be the seam of the cup. For these

9 To make the bottom, I use a cookie cutter that's just larger than the bottom diameter. The cutter is from a graduated set I found at a kitchen supply store.

10 Enlarge the base of the cup not by pinching but by flaring out the edge by turning the finger over the thumb until the bottom matches the diameter of the cutter.

11 Roll out a slab for the bottom, add texture and cut with the cookie cutter. Use a sharp knife to bevel the edge at an angle to remove bulk on the seam.

12 Score and slip the bottom and place it into the flared rim. Pinch the seam with clean fingers. Use a tool to create a smooth surface.

two cuts, the knife tip should point to the left.

I use small masonite bats to handle the cups through assembly, keeping contact with the cup itself to the absolute minimum. When you pick up the cut-out slab from the wareboard, orient the cup so that it is sitting on its lip. Bend the slab into the round, using the seam area and the inside as much as possible to keep your fingers off the texture. Score and slip, then pay particular attention to closing the seam.

When you're working the seam from the inside, run your finger or

tool up, overlapping each stroke across the whole diagonal of the seam. Keep your fingers gently on the outside for support. You should be able to just feel the tool moving on the inside of the cup. While the cup is upside down, only work the seam from the middle to the foot.

Use either a circle template or a cookie-cutter to cut a nice circle for the floor of your cup. For reasons of aesthetics as well as balance, I use one size larger than the bottom of the cone, and enlarge the bottom to fit. Don't pinch the bottom to enlarge. Rather, roll your finger over your

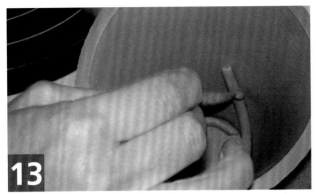

Flip the cup over and nudge a coil into the seam where the bottom is joined to the cup. Smooth the seam with a small brush with springy bristles.

Start shaping the cup using a large throwing stick being careful to overlap each push all the way around.

Add a slab handle. Once the cup is bone dry, finish the rim using an emery cloth and a damp sponge.

thumb gently all the way around the foot a few times, until the base of the cup matches the size of the cutter.

Prepare a small slab with your chosen texture, line up the pattern and cut your circle. Remove the clay around the cutter, then gently press the bottom of the cup out of the cutter. Make a small undercut, which will de-bulk the bottom seam, score, slip, and join. Using a banding wheel, apply gentle pressure with either your finger or a tool to remove excess slip and finesse the seam.

"Touchy Trio." Annie prefers to make cups by hand, reinterpreting the shape of her favorite thrown forms with textured slabs, aspiring to the perfect radial symmetry of Yixing perfection.

Once the bottom is joined and finished from the outside, place another small bat on the bottom of the cup and flip. Now you have to finish working the seam from the middle of the cup up to the lip. If you don't work the seam properly, it will split open when you shape the cup, so don't skimp on this step!

Roll the world's smallest coil, drop it into the bottom of your cup and nudge it into place with an appropriate tool.

Press and work the coil smooth, creating a beautiful transition from the wall to the floor of your cup.

Make and apply a handle to your cup if desired and let dry. Once my cup is somewhere from the hard leather stage to bone dry, I use a piece of emery cloth lying flat on my bench to even out the rim. Then I use a sponge to dampen and a scraper to get to that nice thin lip that feels so good to drink from.

Darting the Duck Butt

Once you get the hang of making your own exquisite cups from the truncated cone, try taking a dart or two here and there for a more sculptural effect. I wanted to make a form that referenced a baby duck while still being functional, so I take out what I affectionately call a "duck-butt" dart.

Line the center of the dart up with the seam of the cup. A clothespin holds the template in place, freeing your hands to cut.

With the knife tip toward the center of the dart, cut each side using an equal and opposite angle.

Remove the dart then score and slip the edges.

Carefully close the edges together. Press gently so as not to mar the texture.

Finish the seam on the inside of the cup.

A baby duck sure looks cute floating on a leaf.

Creating Textured Handles

There's a viable alternative to the drudgery and messiness of pulling handles—making them from slabs. I think slab handles are especially pleasing when impressed with a texture because it adds an extra visual—as well as tactile—zing. Furthermore, there's no waiting for slab handles to set up since they can be made and attached right after a cup is trimmed. I slip, score, then slip, and score through the slip again, to create an interface where the handle joins the cup. Then I set the finished cup in a plastic box overnight.

I first experimented with slab handles while an undergraduate, encouraged to try as many different ways to make handles by my professor, John Brough Miller. Back in '97, when I saw Lana Wil-

son make handles from a thin slab that she then folded over, they really began to make sense. The extra volume created within the slab when folded creates the perfect weight in regards to the thickness of the handle in relationship to the overall balance of the cup.

I've never had a problem with air being trapped within the handle, in part because the seam created by the fold is an informal one. There's no need to slip and score that seam, just let one side rest atop the other. The seam can be put on the inside of the handle, or used as part of the design on the outside. A vent hole can be added—just put it in an inconspicuous place—and knock off any sharpness created before firing!

I make cups in "litters" of a dozen or so. When I

I use a Chinese mallet, which is rounded on one side for roughing out a slab and flat on the flip side for finishing.

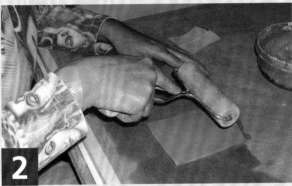

Use the mallet or a roller to get the slab perfectly even, then sponge off.

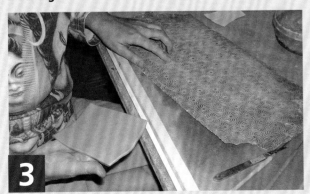

Try anything and everything for texture! This is a piece of rusty tin I found.

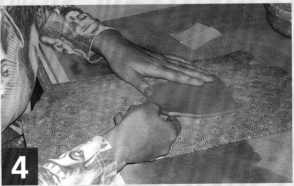

Align the slab with the texture. If clay sticks to your texture tool, clean off and dust lightly with corn starch.

5 Roll the slab into the texture form applying even pressure.

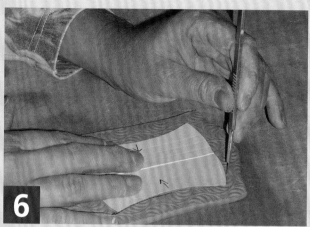

6 Create a template for the handle based on the shape and form of your piece, as well as the texture.

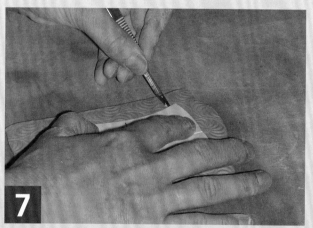

7 Cut top and bottom with the knife perpendicular. Cut the sides at 45° to avoid bulk at the overlap.

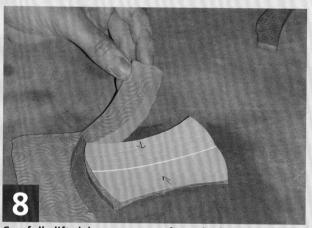

8 Carefully lift slab scraps away from the handle.

change the form of a cup, I'll change the shape of the handle, and also the texture. Every texture bends a different way. Just roll out a slab, then cut it into even strips, impress with different textures, and you'll see what I mean.

I have many different texture tools. The fan or flower texture is a piece of rusted tin I found back in the early '90s on an abandoned farm. I also, like other textural potters, use retired batik blocks—my favorite

blocks were found at a street market in London. These blocks can surprise you, as the negative space often takes on volume and dominates the texture. I also cut apart corrugated craft paper and tape it back together to make corrugations that meet in dynamic angles.

Start with a small piece of clay and make a thin, strong slab (I use a Chinese clay mallet to pound out the slab). Create a template that works with the texture you're going to use

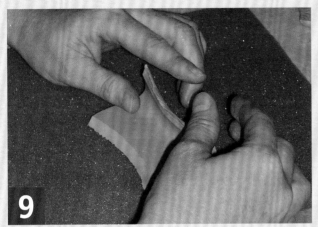

9 Set the slab pattern side down on a soft surface. I use foam pads for this. Start to fold one side into the center (remember to clean your fingertips!).

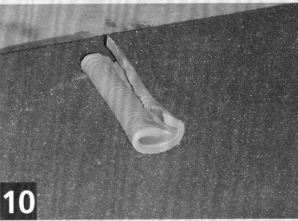

10 Roll in the second side and create an overlap. This is an informal seam—no slip is needed.

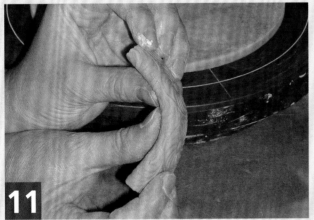

11 Shape the handle then trim to fit the form. Score and slip the handle and the form, then apply the handle.

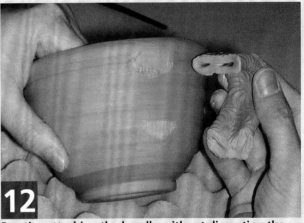

12 Practice attaching the handle without disrupting the texture. It takes a bit to learn the touch.

as well as the size of the cups you've thrown. Align the template to the pattern in the texture and cut the sides with the tip of the knife pointing it in to reduce the amount of clay where it overlaps once you roll in the sides of the handle. Make sure you keep both the area you're working on and your hands free of "crumbs," otherwise they'll embed themselves in, and disrupt your texture. Crumbs tend to become even more visible when you start to shape your handle.

Evolving Style

Cynthia Guajardo's cups reveal the evolution of the textured slab technique taught by Annie Chrietzberg at a workshop, combined with a thrown top to make a unique style geared to her own needs.

When you make a pot, you're participating in a long, ongoing tradition. No pot you make will be perfect, but as you continue your journey in this peculiar field, if you really pay attention, your work will teach you something. Five people who start with the exact same project will inevitably notice different things, and if they follow those threads, they will end up with a style and technique all their own.

Tweaking a Technique

After publishing the preceding cup technique in *Pottery Making Illustrated*, I received quite a few pleas for help with the seam on the side of the cup. At first I explained that, like everything else in clay, keeping that seam together while altering the cup just took a bit of practice. But, as I made my own cups over and over again, I began to notice that I was being generous with the cut on the sides of the template that would make the side-seam, intuitively beginning to allow for the curve that came when I 'bellied out' the cup after assembly. With a bit of experimentation, I modified the templates accordingly, and now, when my cup is put together and ready to alter, the curve that's added by pressing out from the inside is already started in the seam. This not only helps to keep the seam from splitting, but also serves to make members of sets a little more alike than they were before!

Cynthia's style evolved from what she learned at a workshop (left) into a style that better suited her needs (right).

Odd Sources

Ceramic artist Jennifer Merrill-Palethorpe came to my workshop at a time when I was particularly hungry for new patterns, bearing a piece of a gift bag made from embossed paper she had been using as a texture tool. A quick internet search turned up a few sources, and I've used two of them—www.papermojo.com and www.handmade-paper.us.

Embossed paper is a consumable texture tool, but it's not too expensive ($5 or less for a 3×4 ft. sheet). It cuts up easily and can be reassembled into a personal texture-quilt. As a bonus, you can usually pull imprinted slabs from both the front and back of the pattern. I discovered through trial and error that the metallic papers don't last as long as the nonmetallics, and your patterns last longer if you let the paper completely dry out before you use it again, so buy a few sheets, especially for production.

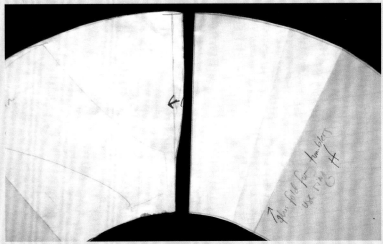

Tweaking the edge of the pattern (left) resulted in less stretching of the clay during the 'belling out' stage.

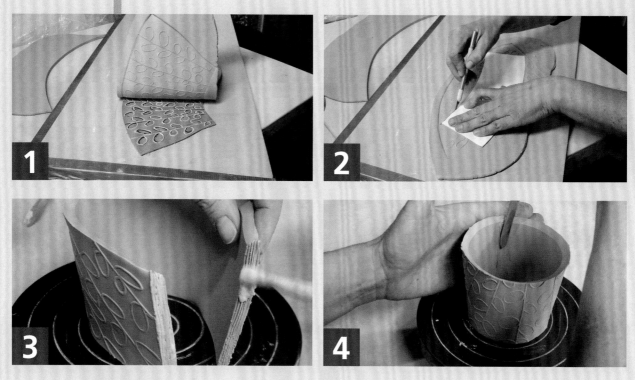

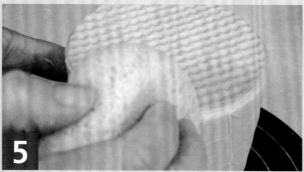

Evolving a Style

Cynthia Guajardo is a ceramic artist in Denver, and I caught up with her one evening as she was unloading a kiln and getting ready for her fall guild sale. I was particularly fond of some new cups she was making, combining the slab cup method with some thrown elements of her own. She told me, "My biggest concern about taking your workshop was that I was afraid that I'd be making 'Annie work,' and I did make a bit of it while I became more acquainted with the technique and using templates."

Cynthia, who is a ceram-o-blogger (http://coloradoartstudio.com/blog) with an avid audience (she starts her day on her couch with her laptop and a strong cup of coffee), says, "I wanted to make a form based on what I look for when buying a mug from someone else: it has to have flat stable bottom to sit on the arm of my sofa where I drink my coffee—no teetering allowed."

Working with templates, she designed a cup with a broader base that still opened outward toward the lip. "Then, as I was working with that design, I decided I wanted an even broader base, so I turned the bottom

into the top. I was heading in the direction of increasing the volume, and was already making some slab vases with thrown tops. I thought the technique would work really well for a cup, too." And it does!

The Evolved Cup

To make a cup combining the slab technique with throwing, Cynthia begins by laying a slab of clay on her linocut texture mat. Using a small rolling pin, she presses the clay into the texture. Her linocuts provide a good amount of relief and create a really nice visual and physical texture (figure 1).

In this demonstration, the texture template is larger than what she needs, so she uses a smaller template and cuts out the required shape (figure 2).

She stands the walls of the cups up on a banding wheel, bottom end up, then scores and slips the side seam (figure 3). She works carefully to join the seam so the texture remains intact. Supporting the seam from the outside, she works the seam from the inside (figure 4).

For the base, she makes another textured slab and cuts out a circular piece for the bottom of the cup. After

Always position tools so that you carve away from your hands and body.

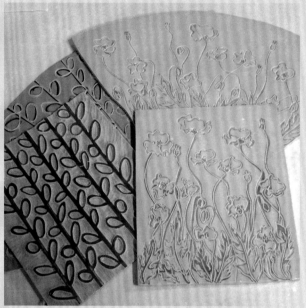

Cynthia carves texture mats from linoleum. Some of the blocks also serve as templates for cups and other forms.

beveling the edge, she scores both edges and attaches it, finishing it off with a sponge (figure 5). A coil is added to the inside seam where the bottom is attached and worked with a wooden tool (figure 6).

To throw the top, Cynthia measures the diameter of the rim (figure 7) then places a small square of plastic on the handbuilt portion to slow the drying. She then weighs out a small amount of clay for the top of her mug and throws a bottomless ring (figure 8). The bottom diameter of the ring is the same as the top diameter of the slab cup. She removes the ring and sets it aside to set up.

Once the thrown element is about

the same dryness as the slab-built piece, she sets it on a piece of rubberized, non-skid shelf liner (unfortunately, BatGrabbers are no longer available); carefully placed clay wads will also work. She then scores the rim, applies paperclay slip to both surfaces, then places the thrown ring on top (figure 9), and gently applies downward pressure.

She uses a sponge to clean up any excess paperclay that squishes out and uses a loop tool to trim excess clay from the thrown ring and evens out the seam on the bottom join. With damp fingers and the wheel spinning slowly, she very gently throws in a downward motion, to make sure the thrown part is securely attached then smooths it out with damp fingers (figure 10).

Cynthia then rolls out and textures a slab to make a slab handle, then sets the completed cup aside to dry.

Making Linocuts

Cynthia had already been creating her own personal patterns and textures before she took my workshop. "Printmaking was my other love in art school," she confessed. She uses a simple and direct printer's method of carving into linoleum, then using the linocut to impress a slab of clay. Cynthia loves printmaking and incorporates some of those techniques into her ceramic work. "Making a linoleum cut and creating your own personal patterns is gratifying and easy," she says, and "the tools and supplies can be found anywhere fine art supplies are sold."

She prefers Golden Cut linoleum she buys online from Dick Blick and adds, "I don't like the battleship gray linoleum or the Easy Cut which I can find locally. Some of my classmates in college even used regular linoleum flooring scraps, which can be acquired for free from flooring stores, building sites, friends and basements." She purchases larger pieces and then cuts them into the desired shape, combining texture tool and template.

For the carving, you can buy inexpensive linoleum carving tools where you purchase your lino mats, but Cynthia recommends acquiring woodcarving tools if you have the budget. "Woodcarving tools are much better than the cheap linoleum carving tools you can find for beginners. Palm grip tools can be found at specialty wood carving and printmaking stores," she said.

The other things you need you probably already have: a pencil, an eraser, a Sharpie, an X-Acto knife and a cutting mat to protect your table. And she offers some wise advice: "Caution! These tools are sharp—always cut away from your body, not just away from your hand and fingers. I say this from experience!" She also says that a bench hook is especially useful for people new to carving linoleum. This Z-shaped piece of metal hooks over the edge of your table, and securely holds your work as you carve. She adds that warming the linoleum briefly in a microwave for a few seconds makes it easier to carve!

Cynthia first sketches her design onto the linoleum with a pencil then holds it up to a mirror to see what the design will look like in clay. Once she's satisfied with her drawing, she goes over it with a Sharpie then proceeds with the carving. She counsels, "if you make a mistake, try to incorporate it into your design. Don't worry about small accidental surface scrapes—they won't show up in clay."

Faceted Teapot

by Jeffrey Nichols

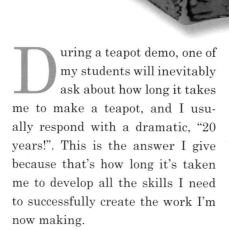

Sanding through the layers of different colored underglazes reveals a beautiful effect like that of weathered wood. A respirator and good ventilation are a must during this process.

During a teapot demo, one of my students will inevitably ask about how long it takes me to make a teapot, and I usually respond with a dramatic, "20 years!". This is the answer I give because that's how long it's taken me to develop all the skills I need to successfully create the work I'm now making.

As clay artists and potters, we're always striving to express ourselves in our own voice. It often takes us years to find that voice because it usually develops out of our experiences, our education, and our exposure to as many different forming and decorating techniques as possible. In addition, everything we read about ceramic art history and keeping up with current trends in the art world also helps to form what we do.

Here I demonstrate making a teapot in my own voice, and you may find it inspiring for helping you to find your own way. Like many contemporary studio potters, I make work that's technically involved, but while my approach is rather complicated, it can be broken down into steps. Hopefully, you can take aspects of my approach and use it to further your own research.

Making the Teapot Body

Begin by throwing a simple boxy form with ³/₈-inch thick walls and a slightly smaller top than base. The simple shape I make reminds me of a Shaker form. Make a fairly shallow gallery in the rim for the lid.

Using a heat gun or hair dryer, dry the teapot body to a soft leather hard then cut it off the wheel. A heat gun is an important tool for my process, but if you use one, remember to handle it safely and follow the manufacturer's instructions.

1 When the form is leather hard, mark lines for the facets.

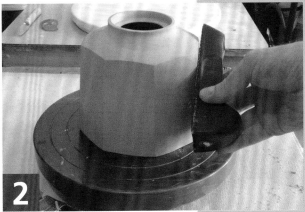

2 Slowly remove clay with a Surform tool to facet the piece.

3 Use a rounded Surform tool to bevel the bottom.

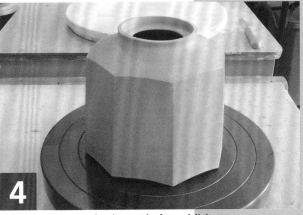

4 A faceted teapot body ready for additions.

Mark lines for the facets (figure 1). Using a Surform tool, create the facets (figure 2). I use a Surform instead of a wire faceting tool or a fettling knife because it gives me more control over thickness and the development of line because you can remove small amounts with each stroke. Next, use a rounded Surform to bevel the bottom of the teapot (figure 3). This helps to visually lift the teapot off the table surface (figure 4).

Handle, Spout and Lid

To create the handle, roll out a coil that's slightly thicker in the middle and tapered on the ends (figure 5). Form it into a **C** or ear shape and place it on a plaster bat to dry to leather hard. Create facets by compressing the handle with a palette knife (figure 6), then attach the handle to the teapot body when it is leather hard.

To form the spout, roll out a tapered coil that's about ³/₈-inch at one end and 1¼ inches at the base. Roll out several spouts in the beginning to get the one that works best for your teapot body. Form the tapered coil into an **S** shape and allow it to

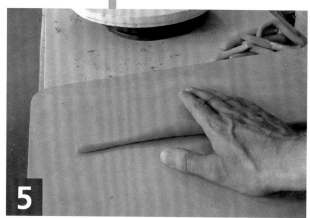

5 Roll out a coil handle slightly tapered at each end.

6 Form the coil into a C and make facets with a palette knife.

7 Attach the handle and spout.

8 Throw a knob and dry it with a heat gun or hair dryer.

set up to leather hard. Use a palette knife to form facets.

Once the spout is shaped, cut it in half laterally, then draw a line about $3/16$-inch from the edge and scoop out the interior of the spout. Re-attach the halves and set the spout aside to set up. Trace the spout opening onto the teapot. Create a series of holes in the teapot body where the spout will attach (figure 7). Slip, score, and attach the spout when it is leather hard. (Note: I've created a video that better illustrates making the spout, which you can view on Ceramic Arts Daily video archive by searching on "teapot spout.")

Make the lid in three stages. First, throw the knob on the wheel (figure 8). With a heat gun, dry the knob to leather hard and cut it off the wheel. Use a palette knife to make the spiral facets. Throw the lid right side up and attach the knob on the wheel (figure 9). Throw a hollow stem and attach it to the bottom of the lid (figure 10). Use a $3/16$-inch hole cutter to create the steam hole in the top of the lid. The teapot is now formed (figure 11).

9

Throw the lid right side up, attach the knob and add facets.

10

Add a flange to the bottom of the lid.

11

The completed teapot is ready for glazing.

Safety with Spray Guns

It is important to maintain a safe and clean working environment while doing this process. Always wear a respirator with a P-100 rating and, if spraying the underglazes, use a spray booth with at least 1000 cfm. I also have a second ventilation system in my studio.

Faceted tea bowl with four layers of underglazes sprayed on then sanded off to reveal the layers, giving the piece a weathered look. A black was applied first followed by red, light blue then medium blue.

Developing the Surface

After years of honing my skills, I finally realized that traditional ceramic processes were getting in the way of my ideas. I wasn't achieving the results I wanted with my ceramic art. Don't get me wrong. I think it's important for potters to have a comprehensive knowledge of the material and possess strong craftsmanship skills, but my true artistic voice didn't develop until I started making work that began with an idea first, not a process.

Inspired by the concept of wabi-sabi, the Japanese aesthetic where beauty is found in things that are imperfect, I began looking for inspiration in non-ceramic surfaces. I found it in surfaces like weathered, painted wood and brick, as well as in nature, within fall leaves and spring flowers. I wanted to create works that evoke the same kind of impact that a Rothko painting does.

The following is the process I developed to replicate these kinds of surfaces. After making a teapot, bowl or vase from earthenware, I bisque it to cone 02 and begin spraying the vessel with multiple layers of Amaco Velvet underglazes. Essentially, I use the Velvets as a high-frit engobe. You can also layer the underglazes by sponging them on if you do not have access to a spray booth. I recommend wearing gloves if you take this approach.

After the underglazes have dried, I begin sanding through the different layers exposing the other colors, as well as the earthenware clay body underneath. Again, remember to wear a respirator! I start with 320-grit sandpaper working to a 600-grit surface. I then fire the piece to cone 04, holding it at maturation for ten minutes to create a strong bond between the clay body and the underglazes.

It is important to apply this surface only to the outside of vessels or in areas that do not come in contact with food or drink. When fired, the Velvets and other underglazes have the durability of a matt glaze, but are not food safe. I then apply a food-safe liner glaze to the parts that will come in contact with food and fire the vessel again. After this firing, I coat the underglaze surface with a food-safe oil sealant (like Salad Bowl Finish, available from home centers) and wax used by woodworkers. This seals the outside surface and makes it fairly durable, but check the instructions on the containers for care and use of these products.

Nichols uses a respirator and a hooded exhaust vent to manage the dust created when sanding his dry surfaces. Below is a surface detail revealing the layers of colors.

Faceted teacup and saucer with four layers of underglaze (black, red, yellow, and orange) applied then sanded. Any number of underglaze colors can be added in any combination—the choice depends on the effect you're looking for.

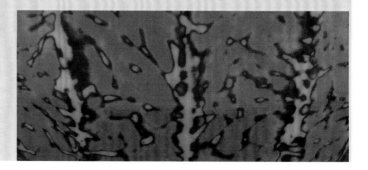

Spherical Teapots

by Ron Korczynski

Spherical teapot,
9 inches in height,
underglaze decoration with clear overglaze fired to cone 04.

Teapots are one of the greatest challenges for any studio potter. Many elements go into their production and all the parts—the body, lid, handle and spout—need to fit together into a cohesive whole. For centuries, teapots have been produced in myriad ways and forms, and like many potters, I initially began making teapots on the wheel. But throwing and putting the parts together was a challenge for me because the forms were too mechanical so I began to experiment with handbuilding. Since I've done a lot of handbuilding using hump molds, this seemed the logical path to take. While the process here uses a spherical form, you'll soon recognize the endless possibilities with other shapes. The teapot form easily lends itself to a wide range of creative expression, and handbuilding a round teapot frees you from the symmetrical mechanized look of the wheel.

Getting Started

Each teapot begins with a slab draped over a plaster hump mold. I make these round plaster hump molds by taking a Styrofoam ball and cutting it in half. Styrofoam spheres are available in a variety of sizes from craft supply stores, and you'll need a 6-inch ball for a modest-sized teapot. Other forms can also work and I use the blue extruded Styrofoam board found at home centers to build up and carve molds. Once the shape is finalized, I glue it to a piece of wood or tempered hardboard that's been cut to shape (figure 1). Tip: You can finish the mold by propping it up and pouring plaster over the top. This gives you a thin, durable, absorbent layer that can be smoothed out when dry and makes a great lightweight mold.

The Sphere

Roll out a slab that's about ¼ to $5/16$ inches thick. Apply toilet paper to the mold as a release and place the slab over the mold.

Trim the bottom, remove and repeat for the second hemisphere (figure 2). Set the hemispheres aside and allow them to dry to the leather-hard stage.

Roll out a coil and attach it to the edge of one hemisphere (figure 3), then attach the other hemisphere using your finger or tool to work the seam (figure 4).

Use a Surform tool to refine the shape (figure 5). Since I do a lot of painting on my surfaces, I use a metal rib to smooth the sphere (figure 6), but you can add different textures at this stage.

Base and Lid

To create a base, one method I like is to use a triangular trimming tool to cut a strip from a block of clay (figure 7). With the sphere resting on an empty plastic container, attach the base and add decorative elements according to your style (figure 8). Of course, design opportunities abound here but bear in mind that all parts on a teapot work to form the whole work.

For the lid, cut a round opening in the top of the sphere and set it aside. In order to have the lid fit only one way, make a small notch in the opening (figure 9). Place toilet paper around the edge of the opening as a separator. To construct the lid, first place a small ball of clay in the notch (figure 10), then add a coil of soft clay to fit into the lid opening (figure 11) so it slightly overlaps the opening. Take the clay piece you removed to make the opening and attach it to the coil (figure 12). Flip the lid over and add a ball of clay to the underside of the lid (figure 13). This will add some weight and balance to the lid to help hold it in place when pouring tea.

Spout and Handle

To form the spout, flatten a cone of clay (figure 14) and form a spout around a brush handle (figure 15). Trim the spout and attach it along with decorative elements to the teapot. To create the handle, I create two "dog bone" shapes and flatten them, leaving some thickness at each end (figure 17). Assemble the handle and add a decorative element if desired. Add a handle to the lid following the same style (figure 18).

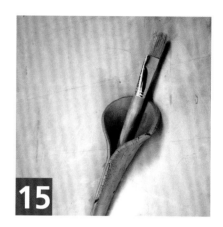

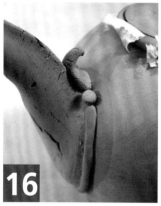

Many teapots can be made using this technique, and the handbuilt sphere can form the basis for a variety of vessels or sculptures. The possibilities are endless.

Altered Teapot

by Cheri Glaser

Wood/salt-fired stoneware teapot, 6 inches in height.

Taking a wood-firing workshop was an eye-opening experience. The total attention and commitment to the process, and the warmth and life of the finished pot were considerably satisfying. After building my own 40-cu. ft. fast-fire kiln, my first pieces emerged with the warmth but not the "life". I had to get to work on the forms and to rethink my production technique. I started throwing on a treadle wheel and using softer clay. I altered the pieces by distorting them as I removed them from the wheel. I found that by throwing pieces without a bottom, I could make a variety of shapes, including squares, rectangles and triangles. Making the bottom separately allowed me to attach it after forming the main body of the pot. My production cycle lasts until I've filled my ware carts with bisqued pots, then I know it's time to gear up to fire the kiln. It takes me two days to glaze, one day to wad pots and wash shelves, and one day to load. It takes between 12 and 16 hours to fire to cone 10 and I salt around cone 8 with five pounds of salt.

Making the Parts

To make a rectangular teapot, I first throw a disk about ½ inch thick that's considerably wider than the base of the teapot (figure 1). After cutting the disk off the wheelhead, I lift it carefully by the edge and allow it to dangle for a moment to stretch

Throw a disk for the base.

Stretch the disk.

Measure the diameter of the rim and flange.

Cut the lid off and squeeze it.

Insert a tapered dowel into a carrot of clay.

Pull the handle around the dowel.

PROCESS PHOTOS: TERRENCE DUFFY

Magic Water

To prevent cracking and separation of parts, I use "Magic Water" in place of water or slip when attaching pieces. To make your own Magic Water, add 3 tablespoons of sodium silicate and 5 grams of soda ash to 1 gallon of water.

it (figure 2), then fling it onto a plaster surface with the finger ridges facing up. This elongates the slab. Sometimes I fling it a second time for a more elongated spiral.

For the teapot body, I throw a cylinder on a bat using 2 to 3 pounds of clay. I open it up all the way to the edge of the bat, then I pull up the walls and form a gallery at the top for the lid to sit in. Once a satisfactory shape has been formed, I carefully measure the inside width of the gallery with calipers. I squeeze plenty of water into the form, which allows the walls to slide easily, then I cut it from the bat with a wire a few

times. After pushing the sides into a rectangular shape with the palms of my hands, I let the form stiffen up a bit while I throw the lid and pull the spout.

The lid is thrown right-side up off the hump. Since I work in a series of six to eight teapots at a time, I throw a couple of extra lids. Using a second set of calipers calibrated to the first measurement, I measure beneath the flange where the lid will sit on the gallery (figure 3). I cut the lid off the hump with a twisted wire, and as I lift it up, I give it a slight squeeze beneath the flange to create an oval

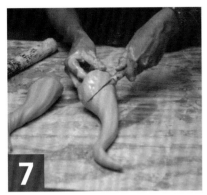

Shape the spout.

Score the slip the parts.

Smooth the interior seam.

Compress the bottom seam.

Prepare the spout for assembly.

Prop the spout until it sets up.

lid (figure 4). If the round measurements are accurate, the parts should fit together after they are distorted into ovals.

I started pulling spouts for teapots and ewers to eliminate the twisting of a thrown spout after high firing. Pulled spouts allow for longer and more fluid shapes, including S-shapes. I start with a large "carrot" of clay and insert a dowel lengthwise through the center (figure 5). A tapered wooden dowel is better than a straight one because it gives the fluid stream a better flow in the finished product. Holding the dowel in my left hand (I'm right handed), I start pulling the clay, with plenty of water, in an upward direction (figure 6). I keep wetting the dowel by pulling it out and dunking it in water. It's important to keep the dowel wet so the clay won't stick to it. I keep pulling until I get the right size spout for the pot I'm working on. For variety, you can twist the clay while pulling. I then slide the spout onto a board where I shape it into an S (figure 7).

Assembly

All the pieces come together on day two. I flip the slab over so the spiral is on the bottom. I place the teapot body centered on the slab and draw

13

Attach the handle.

14

Add coil feet.

around the perimeter, then I score the slab and body, slip with Magic Water (figure 8)) and gently squish them together. I use a chopstick with a piece of foam rubber attached with a rubber band to seal the seam on the inside of the pot (figure 9). I cut the excess clay from the slab and finish off the outer seam, and compress it with a roller (figure 10). Next, the lid is fitted, without too much further adjustment, I hope. If the lid is very shallow, I add a small piece of clay to the back as a catch.

Before adding the spout, I trim the base and carve out the excess clay from the inside of the inside of the spout to create a wider space (figure 11). After cutting the hole from the teapot for the spout, I pinch the edge out a bit to allow greater surface contact with the spout base then score and slip it into place with Magic Water. Prop the spout until it sets up (figure 12). For the finishing touch, I add the handle, which I pull off the pot (figure 13) and sometimes add coil feet (figure 14).

Cane Teapot Handles

by Frank James Fisher

Every teapot needs a handle. As talented potters, we could make a beautiful ceramic handle. But sometimes a teapot needs a little natural wood to contrast the ceramic surface. Wood handles provide a friendly warmth that's inviting and appealing to hold.

There are ready-made handles of wood, bamboo, rattan and cane available through ceramic supply stores. I'm partial to cane for my teapots, either English or Chinese cane. The English cane seems to have a smoother surface as far as blemishes are concerned. The Chinese cane is slightly thicker in diameter and sometimes has a "natural" or rough look to the surface. Because the Chinese cane is considerably less expensive and is completely covered for this project, it's the practical choice. Cane handle styles include the horseshoe, the oval and the square cane.

I've relied on a variety of ready-made handles for years, but I admit to feeling a tad guilty when I don't make the handles myself. After all, I

Teapot with modified cane handle, stoneware, fired to cone 10 reduction. Includes an assortment of ready-made handles, a coil of common cane and a coil of dyed reed.

Teapot with modified cane handle, porcelain, fired to cone 10 reduction.

Teapot with modified cane handle, porcelain, fired to cone 10 reduction.

spent a great deal of creative energy on the body of the teapot only to clip-on a ready-made handle at the end. The results looked fine, but I didn't feel fine. I created a unique custom teapot and used a generic handle.

The answer came through a mix of family and friends. My mother weaves baskets and wove several wonderful handles from willows. As nice as these handles looked, they didn't reflect the tightly controlled aesthetic I wanted for my teapots. A fellow weaver suggested using the ready-made cane handles and adding some innovative cane wrapping. This approach resulted in a refined,

sturdy handle that functioned well and could be customized for each teapot.

Attach the Handle

To begin, attach the cane handle. First, dip the ends of the cane handle in boiling water for a minute to soften the cane. Bend open the flange ends and slip through the ceramic loops of the teapot. Bend the flange back into place against the handle and secure tightly with the woven cane loops. Set aside to dry.

When dry, cut and remove the woven loops and discard. Check the fit where the cane flange meets the cane handle. This transition at

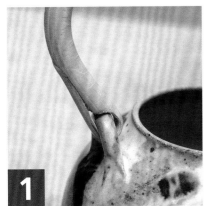

Glued and sanded cane handle.

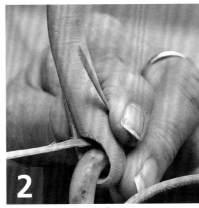

Insert cane through cane handle opening.

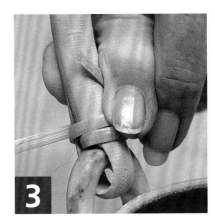

Begin wrapping coils around cane tip.

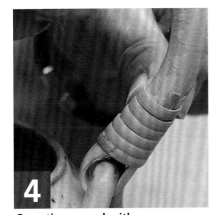

Cane tip secured with wrapped coils.

Align the colored reed ahead of next coils.

SUPPLIES

- Ready-made cane handle
- 6-foot length of common cane, 1 mm.
- 1-foot length of flat oval colored reed
- Bottle of Insta-cure, gap-filling, cyano acrylate adhesive (Super Glue)
- Bottle of Insta-set, rapid-curing accelerant
- Scissors and hobby knife
- Basin of water approximately 8–9 inches in diameter to soak the cane

this juncture needs to be smooth; no bumps where the two pieces of cane come together. You'll be wrapping the cane over this area in future steps and any misaligned joints will show. If there are bumps, sand the transition smooth. Once satisfied with the dry fit, apply the Insta-cure gap-filling cyanoacrylate adhesive and press together. There should be a little give at this point to align the joint perfectly and give the joint a spray of the Insta-set rapid-curing accelerant. Hold a few seconds and everything should be solid and se-

cure (figure 1). Repeat where the handle attaches on the other side.

Wrapping the Handle

Place the lengths of cane and reed into a basin of room temperature water approximately 30 minutes before you begin the next step.

The 6-foot length of common cane should be damp and pliable (so it will not crack). Begin by poking the end through the open bend just above where the cane handle is attached to the teapot (figure 2). Press approximately one inch of the tip along the handle and begin to wrap

6 Secure the end of the reed with several coils.

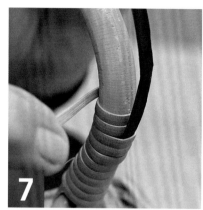

7 Pass two coils under the reed.

8 Pass one coil over the reed.

9 Repeat over and under to the other end. The final wraps over the reed.

10 Trim the reed close to final coil.

11 The last five coils are looser than the previous coils.

the length of cane from the opposite side around the handle and the cane tip (figure 3). This is the hardest part of the project, so don't become discouraged. It is clearly a task designed for persons with three hands. The trick is to have pliable cane and proceed slowly using your finger tips to trap the cane against the handle as you begin to wrap. Once you have three wraps completed, the cane will bind itself into place. Your goal is to get six or seven wraps tightly wound (figure 4). You may need to dip your fingers into the water basin to re-

wet the cane should it begin to dry and stiffen. As you are wrapping, try compressing the coiled wraps together to get a tighter fit. Hopefully the original cane handle will be covered completely by the wrapped cane as you progress along the handle.

After six or seven wraps, it's time to introduce an accent color of reed. Place the tip of the reed on the upper surface of the handle with the tip of the reed in the path of the next cane wrap you will make (figure 5). Bring the cane around to catch just the tip. Continue around with your cane

12 Insert cane through cane handle opening.

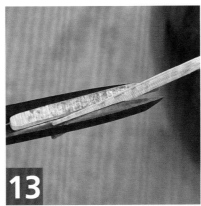

13 Trim the cane end into a narrow point.

14 Threading the cane under the wrapped coils.

15 Twist and tighten the loose coils then pull the cane up tight.

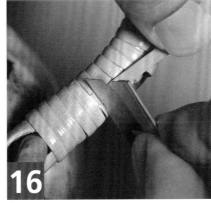

16 Trim the extra cane close to the coils.

wrap for three wraps (figure 6). Stop and take a look at the position of the reed on the handle, you may need to wiggle it back and forth to get it parallel with the curve of the handle.

When satisfied, wrap two more times but pass the cane UNDER the reed (figure 7). Then make one wrap passing the cane OVER the reed (figure 8). Then two more UNDER followed by one more OVER along the entire arch of the handle.

When you reach the spot that is equal to where you began your accent reed on the opposite side, make three consecutive wraps OVER the reed (figure 9). Cut the reed as close as possible to the last coil of cane (figure 10).

Finishing the Handle

The final run of approximately five wrapped coils are done slightly looser than any of the previous wraps (figure 11). When the last wrap is made, take the cane and pass it through the open bend just above where the cane handle is attached to the teapot (figure 12). This is the reverse direction of how the handle was started in figure 1.

To finish the handle, cut the cane with about twelve inches remaining. Trim the end of the cane with scissors to form a long point (figure 13). This will be used like a needle. Place the tip along the handle, under those last loose wraps of cane and thread it up and out (figure 14). As you pull it tight, gently rotate those loose coils in the direction needed to tighten them, moving toward the handle end (figure 15). Take up the slack and pull the needle-like end tighter still. With a little twisting and prodding, everything will snug up tight.

Pull out the Insta-cure gap-filling cyanoacrylate adhesive and place a drop where the cane pokes through the coiled wraps. Give a spray of Insta-set rapid-curing accelerant to harden the glue. Trim the cane from the wraps with a knife blade (figure 16). Now the handle is complete.

Tips

- It's important to wet and re-wet your cane with your fingers during this entire process. Dry cane is difficult to work with and will crack or split.

- Choose a thin cane, 1 mm or less, to wrap the handle. The thinner diameter allows for tighter wraps on the cane handle arch.

- Check the wrapped coils every two or three passes to be sure they are tight against each other. Compress them toward the previous wrapped coils with your fingers.

- Try to match the accent reed color with one of the glaze colors. On this teapot, it was a dark brown. The range of colors available is truly impressive. If you're looking for an unusual color or precise match, dyes are available to stain to your preference.

- You may wish to spray a clear urethane finish on the wood to protect the natural wood colors from stains.

- There are many styles of ready-made cane handles. I shop the internet for best price and lowest shipping. Aftosa has a wide range of styles and sizes.

- All the weaving materials are from a local basket shop, Linda's Gallery in Milford, Michigan. None of the materials are expensive. The cane and reed are sold by the foot.

A wide range of reed colors.

Brush Bottle

by Frank James Fisher

A small bottle with a flared lip used for brushable liquids.

I use white vinegar in my studio to mend cracks in greenware, inspecting every piece before it's fired. But I prefer to keep glass out of my studio, particularly because the tall glass bottle that vinegar comes in is prone to tipping over. I needed a short bottle with a wide base for stability, not unlike an antique ink bottle. My bottle design calls for a larger flared lip suitable for wiping a paint brush, making the bottle useful for any brushable medium.

The bottle is thrown in two pieces: the bottle form and the base platform. Because this vessel uses the narrow-neck bottle form, the centering must be perfect. If the clay becomes even slightly off-center, the lip will flutter, bend or tear later during the compression and forming of the neck. Use well-wedged clay, then pull and compress it at least three times when centering to align the clay particles.

Process

Center a one-pound ball of clay and open it all the way down to the bat. Pull the clay ring outward until the diameter of the bottle base is achieved (figure 1). Slowly pull up and in toward the center—pulling too fast creates an uneven wall. The slightest difference in thickness creates difficulties later when forming the neck (figure 2). Use a wooden rib and press the inside surface against it to remove excess surface clay and remove throwing lines (figure 3).

Slow the wheel and begin forming the neck approximately a third of the way down from the top. Use three pressure points and slowly squeeze inward (figure 4). Run your finger tips simultaneously on the inside and outside of the neck and lip to evenly distribute the clay. Use a chamois to refine and smooth the lip, then compress the clay at the narrow part of the neck using the handle of a needle tool and your fingertip (figure 5). With the basic shaping complete, fine tune it as needed (figure 6).

1 Open clay to full diameter of base.

2 Pull walls up and inward.

3 Even out the walls with a rib.

4 Compress the neck as you collar in.

5 Smooth and compress the inside.

6 Make final adjustments to the shape.

Mark the cut-off line with a needle tool about a ¼ inch up from the bat. The walls should be thin enough at that point. Since there may be excess water inside the bottle, which could cause the form to dry unevenly and crack, remove a wedge of clay at the base and tip the bat to release the water (figure 7).

Make the base with about ¾ lb. of clay. Throw it upside down to create a dish similar to a low-walled dog bowl. Use calipers to ensure that the diameter of the base is slightly greater than the diameter of the bottle (figure 8). Wire off the base from the bat and set both the bottle and base aside until leather hard.

Once the pieces are leather hard, cut the bottle from the bat with an X-acto knife (figure 9), running it along the groove marked earlier by the needle tool. Trim the base upside down, which is actually right-

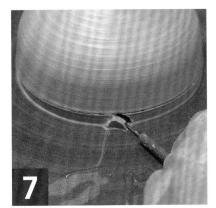

7 Cut out a drain hole at the base.

8 Use calipers to measure the base.

9 Cut the bottle from the bat.

10 Apply slip to scored areas.

11 Attach the top to the base.

12 Clean the seam with a sponge.

side-up in the final assembly. Score the surface of the base and the bottle with an old toothbrush, and apply slip (figure 10). Quickly line up the bottom and top and press them firmly together. The excess slurry will squeeze out of the joint ensuring a strong bond (figure 11). Clean up the seam with a chamois or elephant ear sponge and rotate the wheel until the joint is clean and smooth (figure 12).

Antique ink bottles served as the inspiration for the form of the vinegar bottle.

Functional Ware for the Physically Disabled

by Hanna Lore Hombordy

Bright colors help with visibility.

Some time ago, a caregiver approached me and asked if I could design a special plate for a stroke victim. Though the patient was anxious to feed himself, he was unable to keep the food from sliding off the plate. My solution was to make a plate with a functional "fence" around it (figure 1). The fence slanted inward so that food would fall back onto the utensil when it was pushed against the wall. Food could then be easily pierced with a fork or merely dropped onto a spoon, depending on its consistency. The plate was a success and life became a little less frustrating for the patient. Rethinking the plate made years ago, another solution came to mind recently. The vertical sides could be curved rather than straight, making a smoother path for the eating utensil.

Creating the plate made me realize how the simple daily necessities like eating and drinking could affect the lives of the disabled and how potters can help solve some of the unique challenges they face. Problems might include pain, tremors, limited use of hands, lack of strength and dexterity, and even faulty vision. While the disabled person or the caregiver recognizes a problem, they may not be able to visualize a solution. With direct input from both the caregiver and patient, the potter can help by throwing a series of vessels and testing some variations. Most decisions can be made at the leather-hard or bisque-fired stage.

If the patient is able to grasp it, a knob or handle of some sort could be added to provide further stability (figure 2). A set of smaller dishes would help to separate different foods (figure 3). A special touch might be to make a container for medication (figure 4).

The potter should not be influenced by current conventional styles. A

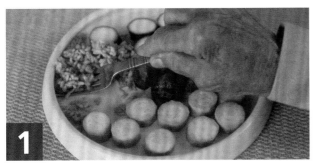

A plate with raised curved sides pushes food against utensils.

A knob or handle aids in adding stability while grasping.

Smaller dishes can keep different foods separated.

Bright colors add a special touch and serve as a reminder to take medication.

person with a disability should use what's practical, not what's deemed proper. Why not make a useful item that's a crossover between a cup and a bowl? Many cultures to this day have multi-use bowls of various types, which are both sipped and eaten from. The orange cup/bowl shown here with a matching cup is made for modest portions, is lightweight, comfortable to hold with two hands, and has a rim for easy sipping yet is wide enough to be used with a spoon or fork (figure 5).

Drinking liquids requires special attention. Spills are a nuisance that should be avoided and a simple mug with several indentations might be easier to grip. You can make the indentations by pressing and stroking

moist fingers against the wall of a vessel (figure 6). An uneven surface, such as a series of carved lines, may also aid the patient in grasping a mug (figure 7).

Handles were designed to protect hands from hot liquids and to help with lifting the cup with one hand. Styles and sizes vary, but a person with one "good" hand would find a smooth, large, generous handle most helpful. A mug with two large handles would aid a person with unsteady hands (figure 8).

A patient who lacks strength due to age or illness might appreciate a smaller-sized mug, lighter in weight, and wider at the bottom to provide stability when setting it back down (figure 9). A lidded con-

A cup/bowl is very versatile.

Small indentations make a cup easier to grip.

An uneven surface makes gripping a cup easier.

Two large handles are easy to grip, even with unsteady hands.

A lightweight mug with a wide bottom is easy to use and set back down.

Lids maintain the serving temperature of food over long periods of time.

tainer keeps food at temperature longer for persons eating and drinking small amounts at a time (figure 10).

For folks with bad eyesight, contrast is important. A white clay with a white or clear glaze provides visibility for the inside of food containers. Bright colors emphasize the outer surface and create a cheerful atmosphere.

My tests were done on white cone 5 clay. Underglazes were brushed or airbrushed onto greenware and a clear glaze was used on all pieces after bisque firing.

Vessels shown here don't offer perfect solutions for assisting the ill or disabled but are meant to inspire potters to further pursue ideas on their own.

Molded Plates

by Amanda Wilton-Green

Making slab plates is a great way to develop basic slab techniques, and using Chinet® plates for forms makes this an easy project. They also make perfect surfaces for exploring decorating techniques.

Making a set of ceramic plates can be fun for the beginner, but is also easily adapted for the more-experienced student. This project presents a direct and fresh slab-forming approach resulting in plates that become great canvases for surface decoration. Materials are simple, inexpensive and readily available.

After only a few hours of work, you can learn how to roll out a good, even slab, and can experience different stages of plastic clay and what the clay is capable of at each stage. You become familiar with simple slump molds and start to consider the form and function of your work. Most importantly, you learn how to handle clay in a direct and intentional way.

These plates become a wonderful surface for finishing, embellishing and glazing. I have expanded this project to include experiments with paper stencils and slip decoration, but that's just the beginning. Try underglaze design work and glazing methods with this project as well. When the project is completed, you'll have a set of plates to use in you home or to give as gifts.

Forming Plates

Roll out a slab to a desired thickness of ¼ to ½ inch. When rolling out a slab, start by throwing it across the table in different directions until it is somewhere close to 3 inches thick. Roll the clay with the rolling pin, taking care not to roll over the edges. Roll two or three times on one side. If you're working on canvas, you'll notice that the clay stops stretching after the first few times because the clay holds onto the texture of

Using a Chinet plate as a template, cut circles in the slab.

Remove excess clay from the rim.

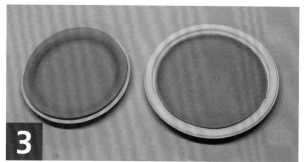

Flip the slab over and place it in the plate.

Press the clay with your hands or press with another plate.

Decorate using any method such as this stencil technique for example.

the canvas. Carefully lift the slab creating as much surface area with your hand as possible, and leave the slab to stiffen to a soft leather-hard stage. The clay needs to be able to bend without cracking, but you don't want fingerprints to show as you manipulate your clay.

Choose the size of your plate. Chinet® brand has dinner, salad and dessert-sized plates as well as an oval platter. Place the plate upside down to use as a template for cutting the slab (figure 1). As you cut, keep your needle tool or fettling knife perpendicular to your work surface to create a square rim.

Remove excess clay and smooth out the rims. Slide your finger across the edge of the rim with firm and consistent pressure (figure 2). The sharp corner of the rim softens without flattening the edge. A damp sponge, chamois or a small piece of a produce bag also works. Stamp or sign the underside.

Flip the clay slab, smooth the top edge then place it into the paper plate, lining up the edges (figure 3). Experiment with pressing the clay into the paper plate with your hands or sandwiching your clay between two plates (figure 4). The clay will have a different character depending on your chosen method.

Allow the plates to dry to a firm leather-hard stage in the bottom paper plate. Remove the clay from the

Equipment and Tools

- Large rolling pin
- Cut-off wire
- Sponge
- 25 lbs of clay with sand or grog to reduce warping
- Fettling knife or needle tool
- Chinet® paper plates.

Note: Chinet® plates do not have a plastic coating and absorb moisture from the clay. Avoid coated and plastic plates.

Interesting Texture Materials

Texture Ideas
Gently roll the following into your plate with a rolling pin:

- Corrugated Cardboard
- Bubble wrap
- Lace remnants
- Mesh produce bags

Stamping Ideas

The following items can be pressed like stamps into the clay but don't do well under a rolling pin:

- Small plastic toys such as animals
- Beaded necklaces (I like the bathtub drain chain, but be careful not to go too deep with this or it can act like a perforation and give your plate a long crack.)

mold to check to see if the plates stack nicely and sit on a flat surface without rocking. Take a moment to look closely at the rim of each plate to do any final shaping they might need.

Decorating Plates

These plates are adaptable to all sorts of decorative techniques at the leather-hard, greenware and bisque stages. The flat surface lends itself to painterly and expressive underglaze or glaze work. These slab plates are simple enough for very young students and satisfying for the adult student.

Slip decoration gives dimension to the plates and students draw on their own creative design ideas for the work. Textured dessert plates with slip inlay use found and inexpensive materials to create a design and a slip in contrasting color to further highlight the design. Paper stencils used with decorative slip can make bold, graphic borders or motifs for your set of plates (figure 5). With a little experimentation and practice, you'll come up with wonderful results.

Making Sets

When you handbuild a set of plates, every artist approaches each plate with a slightly different perspective. The experience of making the first plate, bowl, mug or tile influences the next, as do things as simple as body position and energy levels. We're thoughtful and inconsistent creatures and we can use these characteristics to great benefit when done so with intention. A set of plates can be tied together with a theme, color, position of image, size or concept. Because we're used to seeing sets coming from a factory, the default definition in our minds can be limited to identical objects.

Textured Dessert Plates

Roll out ¼ to ½-inch-thick slabs. Before cutting out the plate, place textured material along one side of the clay slab and gently roll into the clay. Once the material is flush with the top of the clay, peel it away. Clay is great for picking up the most delicate details and is quite beautiful at this stage.

With texture along one side of the slab, place the paper plate templates so that the location of the design will be pleasing on a plate. Remove excess clay and smooth the rims of the plates, working on the top edge and then flipping the clay to finish the bottom edge of the rim. Sandwich the clay between two paper plates and press the clay into the bottom corners of the lower plate. Remove the top plate and paint a generous amount of contrasting slip over the textured area. Leave the clay in the bottom paper plate and let dry until it is a very stiff leather hard. The amount of time varies depending on climate inside the studio. At this stage, use a metal rib to scrape away the top layer of colored slip leaving behind only what is inlaid into the textured areas.

Paper Stencils

Use paper stencils on leather hard clay after clay is placed into the paper plate mold. Each paper stencil can easily be used twice, and with care, up to four times. Keep a copy of the original design. I recommend you prepare by cutting as many stencils as required before beginning the slip work. Trim stencils so that there is about 2 inches of paper around the design. Soak the paper stencils in water until wet but not soggy and then set onto paper towel to remove excess moisture. Position stencils and press down with a damp sponge. Paint slip over the design then remove the paper stencil. If the stencil is too dry to adhere to the next plate, repeat soaking. Sometimes the stencil can be directly transferred to the next plate and pressed with the sponge.

Nesting Bowls

by Annie Chrietzberg

I know I'm not the only overly-involved-with-clay-person out there who brings more things home from a kitchen store for the studio than for the kitchen. So, as I was browsing through a kitchen store, I came across tart tins with scalloped edges and removable bottoms (figure 1), and knew I'd found something that would be fun and easy to use. I bought four of them in graduated sizes thinking: nesting bowls!

To get a square-ish form from a round slab requires removing darts of clay. After experimenting with different dart ratios, I settled on somewhere between a third and a half of the radius. To make the darts template, I traced around the scallops on the cutting edge of the tart tin (figure 2). Ignoring the low points of the scallops, I cut out a circle and folded it along two perpendicular diameters, so that the folds

made a perfect cross. I then found a point somewhere between third and a half way along the radius to cut the darts to. I folded the template in half and cut out a wedge, then used that wedge to cut identical darts all the way around (figure 3). Explore the possibilities of different sized darts different numbers of darts, and different placement of darts. As long as you keep ratios similar from one template to the next, the bowls should nest.

Clean texture tools (figure 4) before using to avoid crumbs of clay that can mar the texture, then dust clean texture tools with cornstarch so that they'll release. Smooth the slab with a soft rib. Leave an inch or so leeway to maneuver if there are flaws in the texture (figure 5).

Place the slab onto the first texture tool (figure 6), gently roll from the center towards the edge in a radial pattern, pushing down just

1 Tart tins with removable bottoms.

2 Create a darts template by tracing around the edge. Ignore the scallops when cutting the circle.

3 To make sure your bowls nest, use the same dart proportions on each template.

4 Clean tools before using to avoid crumbs of clay that can mar the texture, then dust with cornstarch.

5 Smooth the slab with a soft rib. Leave an inch or so to maneuver if there are flaws in the texture.

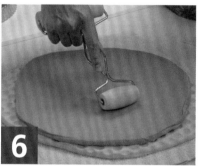

6 Press the clay into the texture, but not so hard that you move the clay and thin the slab.

enough to press the clay into the texture, but not so hard that you move the clay and thin the slab.

Flatten the surface with a big rolling pin (figure 7) then carefully place a prepared texture tool on top of the slab and roll using just enough pressure to transfer the texture, but not so much that you thin or move the slab. Move to a wareboard and remove the texture tools, then flip the slab so the interior face of the bowl is facing up. Use the tart tin to cut through the slab (figure 8).

Slip your hand underneath the rim and place your fingertips at the edge of the slab, gently press the slab free of the cutter. Align the darts and then cut the darts with the tip of the knife angled toward the center of the dart on both sides (figure 9).

Bevel the darts by pointing the knife point towards the center on each side so you'll be switching the angle of the knife for each side of the dart. As always with slab work, score, then slip, then score again to create an interface so the seam stays together (figure 10). You may also want to add a small coil along the seams (figure 11), since you're changing the orientation of the

7

Place a prepared texture tool on the slab and roll using just enough pressure to transfer the texture.

8

With the interior face of the bowl facing up, use the tart tin to cut through the slab.

9

Cut the darts with the tip of the knife angled toward the center of the dart on both sides.

10

Score and slip the cut edges of darts. Carefully lift slab to join both sides of the dart cuts.

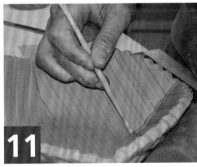

11

Remove the rough edges with a damp sponge, then lay a small coil in the corner.

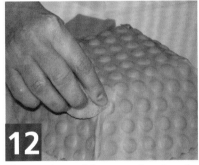

12

Place a piece of foam on the rim of the bowl and flip it over. Work the seams on the bottom down with a damp sponge.

13

Adjust shape and then let dry!

Nesting bowls provide an opportunity for using a variety of textures and glazes.

slab. Use sponges or small pieces of foam to keep the sides of the bowl just where you want them while you work on the join.

After all four corners are well joined, turn the piece over. Anytime you need to turn a piece over, find foam if needed, and wareboards or bats, and find a way to flip the piece without touching it. Run a finger or a well-wrung-out sponge over the backside of the seam (figure 12), eliminating any sharpness and sealing it. Repeat these directions with every size tart tin and template that you have, and you will have a lovely little set of nesting bowls.

With four nesting bowls, you'll want to explore the potential using eight different textures—match textures from the top of one bowl to the bottom of the next, let the textures cycle through the set—there are so many possibilities!

The ABC's of Double-sided Slabs

I've been working with textured slabs for a while now, but only recently got around to eliminating the back, or blank side of the slab. I don't know why it took me so long—but I do find working with slabs with textures on both sides to be very exciting! Here's how you make and use double-sided slabs, along with a few tips to help get you started.

If you have two flexible texture tools, like plastic or rubber mats, pick one and lay it down, texture side up. Dust it with cornstarch (figure A), carefully set your nicely rolled blank slab on top, then roll with the curved end of a pony roller, which seems to push the clay down into the texture rather than enlarging the slab. Then flatten the top with a nice big rolling pin. Dust your second texture mat with cornstarch, lay it on top (texture side down) and carefully roll the back of it (figure B). If you're using a corduroy texture, roll with the lines, not across them. The trick is to apply just enough even pressure to get the texture to print. Rolling carelessly enlarges the slab and leaves 'tracers' of the texture as the slab moves out across it.

When using a brittle texture tool—like a piece of old rusty tin, a bisque or plaster plate, or even a piece of old French patterned glass, you'll need to take more care. I only use those on the bottom, as I don't want to apply my rolling pin to the back of one, because that could mar the surface of my rolling pin or break the tool.

Place a towel beneath the hard texture tool to absorb some of the pressure from rolling so as to keep it from breaking (figure C). If you're using something nonabsorbent, like old patterned French glass, dust it with cornstarch, then lay down your prepared slab, roll, then apply your flexible mat on top of the clay, and roll again.

To remove your slab, peel away the top mat, carefully set a clean wareboard on the slab and flip (figure D). Remove the other texture tool. If your slab is bottom-side up, use another wareboard to flip it again.

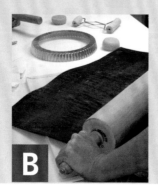
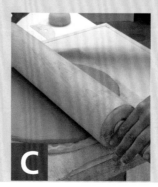

A B C D

Classic American Butter Dish

by Keith Phillips

An American style butter dish, perfect for going from the fridge to the table.

One of the mantras you hear in business is "listen to your customers." As a working potter I've found this to be critical to success. Great ideas come from great customers, and getting feedback from a variety of people who actually use my pots is indispensable. To a functional potter, the function of a design is just as important as the aesthetics, and customers can be a great source for helping you to refine this aspect of your craft.

They can also be a great resource of ideas. I once made a video showing how to make square mugs. Its purpose was to share a technique with other potters and also to give my customers a little more insight into the process of making pots. After seeing the video, I had a customer email me, asking if I could make a regular butter dish, the same way

I made the mug. I had no immediate answer for her, other than I had to try. Having no idea how it would turn out or even what it would look like was the most exciting part of trying it. Thrown forms that get altered into a shape other than circular have a wonderful look and feel—from the graceful throwing lines to the undulating altered form.

After a few days, I had what would become one of my favorite pieces. It was basically two bottomless pots, altered into two long rectangular forms. Slabs were fitted for the top of one form and bottom of the other to create a lid and dish. As much as I liked the final look, making them was not nearly as fun. I found myself measuring the diameters of the thrown forms to be sure that they not only fit around the perimeter of a stick of butter, but also fit well in-

Open the inside all the way to the wheel head or bat and widen the ring outwards.

Once the ring is widened, measure the inside to your preset calipers.

Separate the ring into two thinner rings, as you would for a double walled vessel.

Throw and thin the interior wall into a tall, inward tapering cone. Throw the outer ring into a low, wide, cylinder.

side of one another. I had quite a few dishes that would only fit a half of a stick of butter after shrinking in the glaze firing!

About this time, I saw another video of someone throwing a double walled vessel and a light bulb went off. If I threw both pieces at the same time as concentric circles, they would automatically be sized to fit well when altered. Now, all I had to worry about was the inside diameter fitting a stick of butter, the rest would take care of itself. The efficiency of the process delighted me almost as much as the finished piece.

Note: I assume a 10 percent shrinkage of the clay. Adjust the size of your thrown rings to fit the shrinkage of your clay body.

Throwing the Parts

Before throwing, I pre-set my calipers. If you have one, measure out 4½ inches on your Shrink Rule for the appropriate shrinkage of your clay body. If you don't have a Shrink Rule, measure to 5 inches, which will shrink to 4½ for clay that shrinks 10%. This will be the inside diameter of the inner ring, which becomes the cover of the dish.

It's amazing how little clay you'll need for this piece 1-1½ lb. Center and flatten the clay into a low, wide disc about the same thickness as you

While the clay is still wet, establish the corners. Create the outside corners first.

Create the inside bottom corners next, matching them to the shape of the outside corners.

Slowly push the forms from the inside into rectangular shapes. Alternate between the inner and outer walls.

Continue to gradually push the forms. Eventually you will get closer and closer to the rectangle you want.

would need for throwing a plate.

Open the inside all the way to the bat and widen the ring outward (figure 1). Be careful as the clay might have a tendency to double in on itself. Put a fair amount of pressure on the top of the ring as it moves, so you're essentially squeezing the clay outward.

As the ring widens, measure the inside to your calipers (figure 2). Once the inside diameter matches your measurement, you're ready to establish the two walls. You only need a finger's width in between them. To separate the ring into two, steady your hands on your leg or the splash pan, press one finger down onto the clay around the middle of the ring, and reinforce the pressure with the fingers of your other hand (figure 3). Separate the rings by continuing to press down until you reach the bat.

Once you have the two rings established, throw and thin out the interior wall into a tall, inward tapering cone. Then move on to throwing the outer ring into a low, wide, cylinder (figure 4). This outer ring will become the rim of the "plate" portion of the butter dish.

I've found that tapering the walls in or flaring them out gives the piece wonderful movement when you go to alter it. Have fun experimenting with what happens to different edge

9 Alter the forms evenly from end to end to insure a consistent form.

10 For the top portion of the lid, gently press down on the slab to establish a slight recess.

11 Cut another slab big enough to cover the bottom opening of the tray and apply slip to the bottom of the rim.

12 Flip the rim over, secure it to the slab, smooth the inside joint, and cut off the excess clay.

treatments and how they change when altered.

I also like adding accents to the areas where corners are formed (the top of the interior cylinder) or edges meet. On this form, I've made a simple groove at the top and bottom. Once you're happy with the shape and any decorative marks, take a wire and slice through the bottom, separating the rings from the bat.

Altering the Shape

While the clay is still wet, establish the corners (figure 5). I say "establish" because you're only pinching the corners here, not actually making it rectangular yet. Creating your corners now will help prevent

cracking at the corners when you alter the form later. Also, make a rounded corner rather than a sharp corner to help prevent cracking. Create the outside corners first, then create the inside bottom corners (figure 6).

Note that I did not establish corners at the top portion of the lid. This is because I'm going to keep it an oval shape. The lid ends up transitioning from a rectangular form at the bottom to an oval one at the top.

The timing on the next part of altering is important. You want the clay to be soft, but not so soft that you leave finger prints. You don't want it leather hard or so stiff that it won't bend without cracking. I find

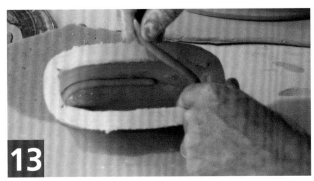

13 Rest the lid on a piece of foam to smooth and reinforce the inside of the lid.

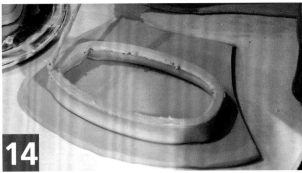

14 Flip the leather hard top over and cut off the excess clay, following the line around the curve as a guide.

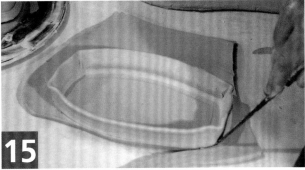

15 Add slip around the edges, slide it into place on the lid and smooth the joint.

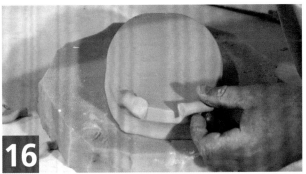

16 Add feet or other accents to the bottom of the dish to elevate it visually.

if I can touch it without a leaving a print, it's ready for altering. Kristen Kieffer has a great term for this clay state—suede. Use a wire tool to slice the forms from the bat again.

Slowly begin pushing the forms from the inside into the rectangular shape. Move the outer wall a little, then the inner wall (figure 7). Slowly alternate between the two. Eventually you'll get closer and closer to the rectangle you want (figure 8). Alter the lid and dish rim evenly from end to end to ensure a consistent form. This photo shows the altering pretty close to completion (figure 9).

Some of my favorite elements of this piece are the throwing lines, which create a wonderful curve once the form has been altered. It's always reminded me of a sheer line on a classic sailboat. Set it aside to stiffen up to leather hard.

Next, you'll need to roll out two slabs, one for the top of the lid, and the other for the bottom of the dish.

Adding Slab-built Elements

Cut a piece from one of the slabs that's big enough to cover the top of the lid and lay it on the opening. If both sides of the slab are free of canvas or fabric texture, then the slab's orientation doesn't matter. If there's texture on one side, place whichever side you want to see face down.

Gently press down on the slab to establish a shallow recess (figure 10). When flipped right side up later

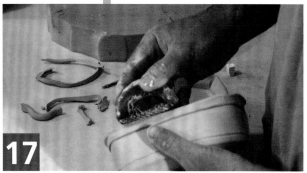

17 Use a rasp or Surform to trim the bottom edge of the lid so that it is level.

18 Attach a handle to the lid. When drying, go slowly and keep lid on the dish.

on, it will have a nice, graceful pillow shape. Leave the slab inverted on top of the lid until it's leather hard, then take the slab off and flip right side up. Cut off the excess clay, following the line around the curve of the pillow shape as a guide (figure 11). The resulting shape won't be an exact match to the opening on the lid because it's a reverse impression, but it will be close enough.

Add some slip to the edges of the top slab and slide it into place on the lid, smoothing at the joint (figure 12). I always reinforce joints with a coil where clay memory will try to pull the joint in opposing directions. Add some more slip to the inside of the lid and gently press in a coil, trying your best not to ruin the nice fair line of your top (figure 13).

I don't use a coil on joints where clay memory will pull at right angles. That is, if the pieces are going to drag against each other, I've found a coil isn't needed. I also use slip that has paper pulp in it, for attaching pieces of clay—thus you don't see any scoring marks. To make paper slip, use a blender to mix a ratio of ½ paper and water and ½ clay slur-

ry by volume. If you're hesitant to try this, score the surfaces and add a reinforcing coil to the base.

Cut a slab big enough to cover the bottom opening of the plate rim and liberally apply paper slip to the bottom of the rim (figure 14). Flip the rim over, secure it to the slab, smooth the inside joint where the wall meets the bottom and cut off the excess clay (figure 15).

Rest the lid on a piece of foam to smooth the bottom of the dish. The foam helps keep pressure off the corners while touching it up. At this point, you can also add feet to the bottom dish to elevate it visually (figure 16).

Finally, clean up the forms and add little details. Trim and clean up the inside and bottom of the lid. Use a Surform to trim the bottom edge of the lid so that it is level (figure 17). Since the lid went from circle to square without trimming, the ends will have a tendency to curve up, creating a rocking horse effect. Lastly, attach a handle to the lid and allow the form to dry slowly with the lid placed on the dish so that if they warp, they warp together (figure 18).

Stilted Bucket

by Jake Allee

Stilted Bucket, 9 inches in height, thrown and altered composite form, oxidation fired to cone 9.

Presentation is everything! Imagine yourself arriving at a party with a six pack of your favorite Mexican beverage hanging from one hand and the belly of a stilted bucket loaded with limes in the palm of the other. Grasping the ceramic piece on the underside enables you to give your host a hearty hug with hands full!

The Stilted Bucket is a product of several elements within my creative process. One of the primary elements is historical inspiration, and, after looking at many examples of Chinese Chou period bronzes, I began to think about how I could change the orientation of my forms to construct new work. Many bronze pieces have a combination of geometric and organic elements with an angular quality that creates interest within the form, and I wanted to inject this into my repertoire.

Deconstructing Chinese forms in my sketch book, I realized that many of these pieces stand on tripods that lift the forms in a manner that makes

Throw a basic cylinder without a bottom.

Mark an evenly spaced grid around the exterior.

Press out the form with your finger.

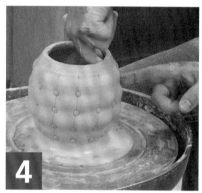

Press in balls of clay at the intersections of the grid.

Throw a disk and compress it.

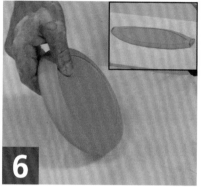

Stretch the disk into an oval.

me want to put my hand under them and lift them up. I also realized that most of the textures created from altering clay appear on the sides of my pieces, and the light bulb in my head turned on. How could I create a form that would make the viewer want to interact with it in the same way that I wanted to handle an ancient Chinese bronze on a tripod.

The Stilted Bucket is composed of three basic thrown forms. The first is a bulbous cylinder that is marked, altered and sprigged. The second is a thick disk stretched into an oval. The last is a bottomless, wide cylin-der with a clean lip and attention given to the base. After creating these pieces, they're cut apart and reused for assembly. Do all the throwing at the same time to ensure even moisture content in the components.

Process

Throw a basic cylinder without a bottom (figure 1). Pay extra attention to centering because any flaw is reflected in the final form. After creating the profile, carefully mark an evenly spaced grid around the exterior (figure 2). The next step exaggerates the form and the end result is larger in volume.

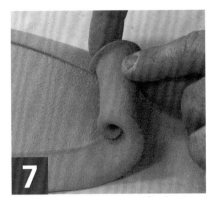

7 Roll the edges over to eliminate any sharpness.

8 Throw a wide bottomless cylinder.

9 Trim excess clay from the bottom of the bulbous form.

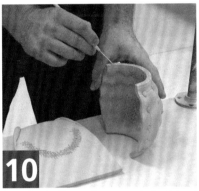

10 Cut the bulbous form and stretched disk in half.

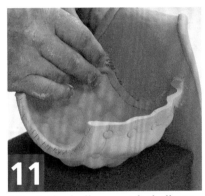

11 Attach the bulbous underbelly to the stilts.

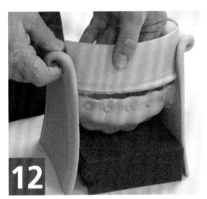

12 Cut away a section of the wide cylinder, and attach it.

Starting from the bottom and working to the top, press out the form with your finger using the marks as a guideline (figure 3). Make small balls of clay and press them into the clay at the intersections of the grid (figure 4). This pushes back in and emphasizes the alteration. Trim excess clay from the bottom. Set aside and allow it to become leather hard.

Throw a 1-inch thick disk and compress it, but end the compression about ¾ inches from the edge (figure 5). This creates a line that later relates to the pot's design elements.

Keep the outer edge profile smooth then undercut the disk (inset).

Immediately remove the disk from the wheel and stretch it into an oval by throwing it onto a canvas surface (figure 6). Make sure the piece hits the table at an angle so the disk stretches. The clay should make a "wisp" sound instead of a "WHAM!" when it hits the table.

After stretching the disk, roll the edges over to eliminate any sharpness (figure 7). This also creates a relationship between the curled area and the handles that will be attached later.

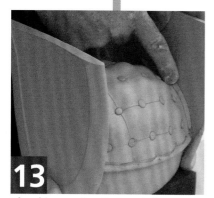

13 Blend in small coils to reinforce all joints.

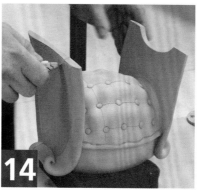

14 Cut a curve in the base of each stilt.

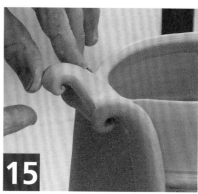

15 Attach handles to the top of the stilts.

Throw a wide bottomless cylinder (figure 8). Mimic the curve created by the side of the bulbous altered cylinder. Shape and compress the lip. Finish the base with an old credit card with a curved notch cut into it. This creates a line that relates to the profile of the other edges. Set aside to stiffen up.

Trim excess clay from the bottom of the bulbous form (figure 9). The piece should be symmetrical top to bottom and left to right. Cut the leather-hard bulbous form and stretched disk in half (figure 10). These become the belly and the stilts respectively. Prepare for assembly by scoring the pieces.

Place the bulbous underbelly on a piece of foam and attach it to the stilts (figure 11). Reinforce the connection on the interior with a small coil that is blended in. Attach the other stilt. Cut away a section of the wide cylinder, and attach it to the rim of the bowl (figure 12). Remember to always leave more clay than you think you will need when cutting this piece.

Blend in small coils to reinforce all joints on both the inside and outside of the piece (figure 13). Continue to rest the piece on a block of foam to protect the stilts and bowl. Cut a curve in the base of each stilt (figure 14), but pay attention to the relationship of these curves to the established composite form.

After addressing the details on the underside, pull two short handles and attach them to the top of the stilts (figure 15). Curl the handles to mimic the top of the stilt. Dry the piece under plastic for several days.

Triple Stilted Bucket, 6½ inches in height, thrown and altered composite form, soda fired to cone 10. An architectural piece designed to elevate food in the extravagance of the standard smorgasbord spread. This piece operates under the assumption that not everyone likes chocolate pudding mixed in with their creamed corn.

Sketching it out

I always begin a new piece by sketching because it allows me to change and rearrange proportions within the form before I produce the actual clay piece. This is an important step because time making clay objects is very valuable to me and I want to be as efficient as possible with this time. A composite form relies on all the parts fitting correctly, and, although clay can be quite forgiving at times, too many components in the final piece can open up the possibility of a piece looking over worked. After several sketches, I'm mentally clear on how to approach the piece so I take to the clay.

Chip and Dip

by Steve Davis-Rosenbaum

After a long day in the studio, I often unwind and relax by watching a movie while snacking. Going to the kitchen, I collect the appropriate pots, bag of chips, dip and drinks. Carefully juggling all these items back to the couch, I sometimes spill dip and chips along the way. After cleaning the mess, I can finally relax.

Practical issues based around comfort, convenience and food are a rich source of inspiration. As a potter focusing on function and form, what could I create to ease the schlepping of my chips and dip? Ideas, research and designs begin by asking questions about function and form that assist our special needs or uses. By choosing function as a guiding limitation, I'm free to explore alternative forms, evaluating them by their function, proportion, line, shape and space (both negative and positive). My process for developing a new form begins with drawing preliminary sketches, and experimentation and play in the studio, which results in a 3-D "sketch book" of shapes and forms.

Before beginning the design for my Chip and Dip, I had been creating multiple vessel forms for many years. In addition, I had researched the historical multiple vessel forms from a variety of cultures throughout time. Over the ages, potters have had the impulse to put two pots together creating new forms and uses for them. For example, multiple vessel pots have been found as early as the Neolithic period in locations such as China, Peru and Iran. Many of these pots had a variety of functions in religious and marriage ceremonies, as decoration or for daily use. My

multiple vessels also revolve around a defined function and the relationships between the individual pots when placed together creating new space, line and volume. Successful pots are created by understanding the function and constantly evaluating how the pieces go together.

The challenge here is not to just remake the Chip and Dip, but to use it as a jumping off point to inspire new forms and designs.

Designing a Chip and Dip

When deciding on size, envision the amount of chips and the quantity of dip required for the chips before you start making bowls. I usually make five sets bowls and straps then mix and match the parts till each becomes aesthetically pleasing. If needed, I go back to the wheel and remake bowls.

Throwing the Bowls

I throw all the pieces in the same sitting and create 4–5 sets at a time. Depending on the firmness of the clay and rate of drying, I plan my studio schedule to have a 3–5 day period to work on the multiple forms. I also throw multiple parts for each Chip and Dip, allowing myself to make critical aesthetic decisions during assembly. By working on several Chip and Dips at the same time, new ideas develop while I work on each pot. This design requires two bowls for the construction/assemblage, which should be proportional to each other and, when placed side by side or held on top of each other, give the sense of belonging together.

Allow the bowls to set up and reach the soft side of leather hard. Completely finish the large bowl by cleaning the rim and trimming the foot before adding any other parts. Cut and manipulate the small bowl to fit the shape of the strap later.

Making the Strap/Handle

Throw the strap as a donut, opening the clay all the way to the wheelhead and pulling the walls of the clay to the edge of the bat (figure 1). To finish the walls of the strap, taper the rim (figure 2). Cut and let set up to the soft side of leather hard. Turn the donut upside down and trim

Mark the location of the handle.

Score the rim.

Check the fit of the handle.

Attach the handle to the large bowl.

Add a support of leather-hard.

Cut the small bowl to match the curve of the top of the strap.

Attach the small bowl after scoring and slipping edges of bowl and handle.

Blend in a coil around the outer seam to help secure the bowl.

the bottom of the strap then shape it to match the thrown end. Place the strap on a canvas and cut one end, then move each end to create a shape for the desired design (figure 3). Remember, the top will hold the smaller pot and the shape needs to

allow hands to enter and leave with chips. Let stand to set up more so it can stand on its own.

Assembly

Since there are multiple pieces to the Chip and Dip, timing and attention to the attachment areas is very impor-

Much of Steve Davis-Rosenbaum's pottery originates from the basic human joys
of eating and cooking with all the overtones these activities evoke: fireside,
nourishment, camaraderie. For Steve, beautiful pottery dishes are synonymous
with love of food and its presentation, and his pottery production focuses on
everyday dishes for use in cooking, dining and home decoration.

tant. Before the pot can be assembled, all the pieces need to be at the correct stage of leather hard. To control the drying time, the pot stays covered in plastic until the desired firmness is reached. Sometimes spraying pieces with water and covering to maintain correct firmness is necessary.

When the pieces are ready, mark the location of the handle on the large bowl (figure 4), score the rim (figure 5). Shape the handle making sure the ends of the strap are wide enough to straddle the large bowl (figure 6). When the handle can stand on its own, score and slip the ends and attach it to the large bowl (figure 7). Using a soft sponge, chamois or fingers, stretch the strap (like pulling a handle) into shape to change the tension of the clay and prevent warping and twisting. Support the handle in the center with a prop made from leather hard clay (figure 8). Place a piece of paper between the prop and the clay parts to ensure easy removal. With the prop still in place, hold the small bowl up to the handle, making sure the shape and proportion work well. Cut the bottom edge to match the

curve of the top of the strap (figure 9). Rework the tension, alignment and shape of the strap and check all previous attachments.

Attaching the Handle

Score and slip the edges of the bowl and handle before attaching the small bowl to the handle (figure 10). Place a coil around the inner and outer seams to help secure the bowl. Be sure to work in the clay and blend it so the coils disappear. After the bowls set up to leather hard, add handles to top bowl and trim the rim of the large bowl. I find that this visually finishes the form creating one new form from many parts. Make sure the strap can support the top bowl and will not lean over. Check it often and adjust as it dries. Clean rims and attachments. Cover and let the piece dry slowly.

Finishing Touches

Go back to the attachment of the strap and add coils of clay to blend in the edges and round the rim (figure 11), leaving no gaps or unfinished edges. Let the pot dry slowly to minimize warping and leaning.

Covered Jar Set

by Steve Davis-Rosenbaum

PHOTO BY JOE MOLINARO

This covered jar set
illustrates the fluid
lines obtained by
joining two forms.
The form is enhanced
by the shape of the
handle, the lugs on
the sides and the sur-
face decoration.

While working as a resident potter at Berea College, in 1998, I produced utilitarian pottery for the college's retail and wholesale outlets. My throwing list included small covered jars, usually for creamer and sugar sets, which were thrown in series of fifteen to twenty. As my second ware board of covered jars was filling up, I glanced over at a grouping of previously thrown jars. From the vantage point of sitting on my treadle wheel, two of the jars were "visually" connected. My eyes kept returning to this view on the ware board and my thoughts turned to questions:

- "Why not connect these jars together?"
- "What will happen to the form and function?"
- "What will I do about the lids and knobs?"

These questions lead me to actually connect the jars and to continue developing the form.

This moment of listening to my "inner potter" brought an opportunity for change. Moments like these are when ideas are filtered from the subconscious. They're always with us but all too often we choose to not listen. However, this time, I took the opportunity to leave my scheduled work and developed what I saw while working at my wheel. After completing a series of ten double-jar sets, I began to reflect on the resulting series:

"Where did this idea come from?"

"Where else had I seen combined vessels?"

The Search Begins

In my search for images of combined vessels through some of my favorite books, I found a little black and

Throw two identical jars. It is easier to match jars when you make a lot.

Create a gallery for the lid to sit in.

Make lids with a slight inward bevel on the rim.

After trimming, attach the forms by adding a coil between them.

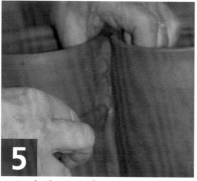

Push the two forms together and smooth the seam.

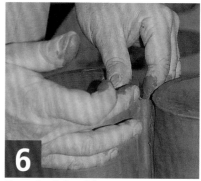

Turn the joined forms over and finish working the seam.

white photograph of a double jam jar with horizontal straps around the belly made by Michael Cardew. The caption read "modeled after Jam-Jar Set by Hamada." Though I was unable to find an example of Hamada's combined vessels, I discovered a wealth of historical examples from around the world.

Through the years, I've continued to study combined vessel forms and their function. What I've observed is the overwhelming number of examples found in all cultures and continents where potters found the need, or impulse, to place two or more vessels together creating a new form. These types of pots occur very early in ceramics history and reoccur throughout time. One unifying element found in these combined vessels is the desire of the potter to retain the essence of the individual vessel within the new form.

Creative Accidents

I realized something about the creative process and how subconscious influences impact my work. Previous to making my first combined vessel, I believe that through reading and studying images, I had stored information in my mind and allowed it to "incubate" over time. These subconscious influences filter into

7 Pull a handle or roll out a coil for the handle and allow to set up.

8 Fit the handle across the lids and secure with slip.

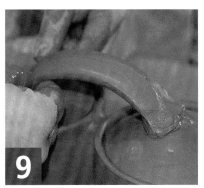

9 Work the handle until the desired shape is achieved.

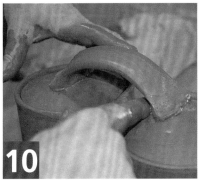

10 Add small coils to complete the join between lid and handle.

11 Add lugs then cover lightly so the moisture can even out.

12 Stretch the handle over the next few days to avoid cracking.

my work when I least expect it, and when I am least conscious of "the act of making"—the act of being in the here and now. Some refer to this as "creative accidents" that happen just by being in the studio.

Making the Connection

Typically, my work is first inspired by a utilitarian need followed by the development of the form—but the double jars sets were different. The jam jar sets became sugar and Cremora® sets. One of my interests in this form was the problem of how to unite the lids to parallel the joining of the form. The idea of connecting the lids with one handle allows the user to remove both lids with one hand, using the other hand to serve condiments on their plate.

As I developed the covered jar sets, the functional aspects of the pots became secondary to form due to increase in scale or an increase in the number of vessels combined. As the jar sets became larger in scale they became less functional and their intimacy decreased. Not being able to easily handle or pass them around a table resulted in a distance between the pot and the user. My interest in making pottery is its use in the kitchen or at the table. Visualizing the table as my

This covered jar set fired in a salt kiln reveals some of the variation possible with just two forms attached.

pedestal (rather than the mantel), I returned to making intimate combined vessels.

In many ways, building multiple pots is like a puzzle. When you begin, there's a variety of individual pieces. When assembled, the resulting form connects in a way that preserves form and maximizes function.

Beyond the Double Jar

In addition to the double jar sets, I developed other combined condiment servers, usually combining two or three vessels. The idea of placing and connecting pots in relation to the shapes being created or eliminated, presents the potter with limitless alternatives.

Working within the boundaries of utilitarian pottery and being open to what I see and what unexpectedly happens in the studio allows open-ness to experimenting with form. The ability to say "what if" while throwing, finishing or decorating is where many ideas are discovered and developed. Thinking about function in my daily life has guided my desire to create new forms.

My guiding creative boundary is function. Having function as a central focus requires an understanding of how food, kitchen objects and other items relate visually and functionally to the ritual of eating. This knowledge informs my understanding of how to develop forms to accommodate complex utilitarian needs. The desire to put individual forms together to create combination vessels is to move my work beyond basic forms created on the wheel. This broadening perspective on my work constantly challenges my views on form and function.

Condiment Server

by Gwendolyn Yoppolo

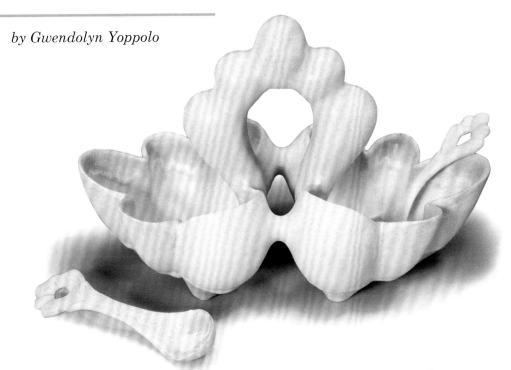

Condiment server, 12 inches in length, hand-built stoneware, gas fired to cone 10.

Condiments and spices are some of the most concentrated, powerful flavors in the kitchen, and I enjoy the challenge of presenting them in interesting ways. The doubled forms on this serving dish imply a complementary relationship between two distinct items being served. The softly sculpted bowls accommodate the spooning of the contents, and the handle connects the forms while creating a negative space for the eye to enter into.

Making the Bowls

Begin by throwing two similar bowl shapes and trimming them to an even thickness. Design your form and create a paper pattern to use as a guide for cutting the round forms (figures 1 and 2). Next, take the soft cut shapes and push, pull and pinch

them into a form to use as the base form (figure 3). Pay attention to the underside since the spines that define the curves grow out from a point underneath (figure 4). Wet and wrap the rim and let the forms rest under plastic overnight (figure 5). If the bowl is still fairly soft, support it with scraps of cut clay so it won't lose its form. Tip: Perform work on top of a piece of foam so that the rounded curves on the underside of the pieces do not lose their definition.

Once the base has set up so that it's stiff enough to support additions, add coils to the rim to build height and shape the edge. As you coil, smooth and compress the clay using a metal rib (figure 6). The newly built walls are left to set up before the edge is shaped and smoothed (figure 7). Notice how the support for a handle begins to grow from the center of

1

Trace the paper pattern onto the bowl form.

2

Remove the contoured shape.

3

Push, pull and pinch each base form.

4

Define the bottom spines.

5

Wrap the edge to let the form rest overnight.

6

Add coils and rib smooth.

7

A completed bowl with finished edge and handle base.

8

Form hollow feet, blend them into the base (A) and make an air hole (B).

9

Create a template for the handle.

the form. If this is built along with the rim, the clay is given a chance to shrink with the bowl, which reduces cracking in this potentially stressed area of joining.

After the rim sets up, make small hollow feet to attach to the underside. Once smoothed in, they're given holes for ventilation (figures 8). After the feet have stiffened, turn the bowls upright.

Making the Handle

Design and cut a paper pattern for the handle, considering the relationship of the handle's form to the

Cut out two handles from the template and shape each one.

Allow the halves to stiffen, then apply slip.

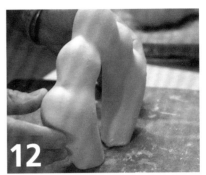

Finalize the contour, then allow to set up.

Make spools for joining the bowls together.

Join the handle to the assembled bowls.

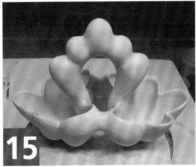

The completed form with all parts blended together.

Forming the bowl of the spoon.

A formed spoon with curve supports.

overall dish form and to the negative space between the pieces (figure 9). Create a few designs on paper, then make two or three handles in clay so you can choose the best one. After determining the pattern, cut two handles from thin slabs of clay and round them out on a piece of foam (figure 10). Concentrate on creating a volume inside the handle that will feel pleasing to the hand. Slip the edges of each half to keep them wet (figure 11), allow the halves to stiffen slightly, then press them together tightly and smooth the seam. Use wooden tools or a metal rib to

Working with Porcelain

A few years ago, I swore off working under the clock in the studio. Since then, my approach has been to do whatever I feel a piece is requiring of me without worrying about hours, days or even weeks. Art making has its own time, and we must respect its pace if we are to keep up.

While you can make this piece more efficiently using molded forms, I enjoy the spontaneity and open-endedness of hand forming too much to deny myself the luxury of touching the clay in a sensual way while I'm building. This is much slower than watching paint dry. The process involves cycles of roughing forms out, followed by letting the clay set up to a point where further refinement can take place.

I use a commercial porcelain clay because of its working properties, smoothness and bright color. Porcelain has a unique quality of setting up to offer a resistant workability achievable with the addition of a little water. Handbuilding with porcelain, however, offers certain challenges. In addition to tips provided in the instructions, here are some general pointers:

- Anticipate the movement of the porcelain in the kiln by compressing clay in the direction you want it to move, by avoiding unnecessary bending of your forms, and by stretching and overstretching added pieces before attaching them.
- Work fairly wet to join pieces together. Make sure all pieces to be joined have a similar moisture content so that they will shrink the same amount.
- Dry work very, very slowly. Water can be redistributed within a form by wrapping the form tightly in plastic and letting it rest. After attaching pieces together, let the form rest overnight or longer in this type of water-equalizing chamber to even out its moisture content.
- Wedge some fine molochite into your clay body to reduce shrinkage and help control cracking.

give the final contour to the handle (figure 12). Allow the handle to dry to approximately the same consistency of the bowls for joining.

Assemble the Bowls

I enjoy the dynamic interaction between the bowl forms and consider this tension while adding small spool-shaped connectors (figure 13), which give the impression that the forms have somehow grown together. Smooth the join then poke a hole in one of the handle bases for ventilation. Before joining the handle, stretch it slightly in and out so that it doesn't pull too hard on the bowls as they dry and are fired. Join the handle to the base, again considering how to create a feeling of growth between the forms (figures 14). Once the form is completed (figure 15), do not move it until it is bone dry. This is important to avoid warping and cracking. Ideally, wrap the pot in plastic for about a week for slow drying.

Making the Spoons

Cut the spoons from a thick slab of clay. Shape the bowl of the spoon by using steady pressure strokes of your thumb, while your other hand supports and guides the rim into place (figure 16). The angle of the bowl in relation to the handle is important—the bowl of a ladle is more of a right angle to the handle while the bowl of an eating spoon is more in line with the handle. For this serving dish, use an angle between the two that sits nicely in the bowl and is good for spooning contents out and serving them.

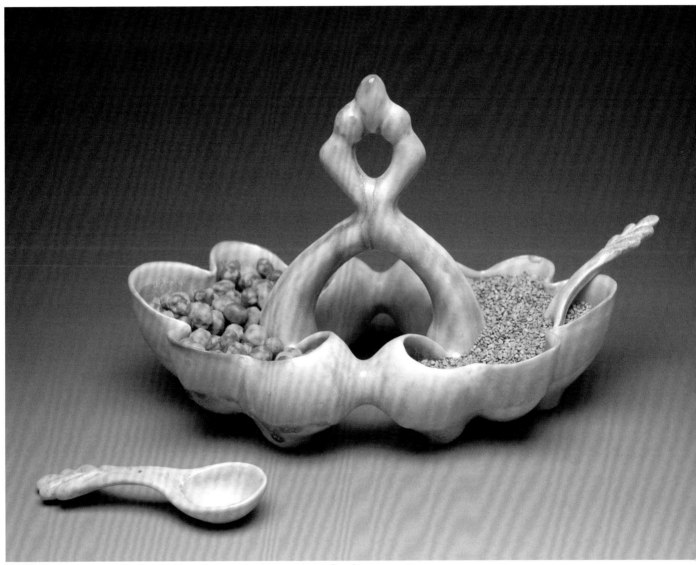

Condiment server, 10 inches in length, handbuilt porcelain, fired to cone 10.

Smooth the handle edges then carve and model the end of the handle to reflect the forms found in the related dish. Let the spoon set up before treating the back in a similar manner. While finishing the handle, give direction to the curve in a way similar to that used when pulling a handle for a mug. Finally, create supports from the same clay body (figure 17). I use this prop for drying and firing the spoon, and when glazing, I choose not to glaze the back sides of the spoons so that these supports will ensure that the spoons will not lose their intended curves.

Handled Platters

by Michael Guassardo

Platter on the left, heavily dipped in a blue cobalt and iron glaze; the one with the fruit, in a tenmoku glaze with an iron and rutile decoration, both were fired to cone 9 in oxidation.

A handled platter is ideal for fruit and salads, and for serving. Provided you are using the proper clay body, you can also use it as a baking dish, as long as it is preheated along with the oven and not taken over 200°C or 390°F.

Platters look deceptively simple to make, as creating one involves very basic throwing, but the larger scale translates into specific technical and design challenges. The form needs to be well constructed so that it survives the drying and firing processes, as well as years of use later on.

Because the platter form is so large, it will be a focal point on the table. In order to integrate all of the parts, the character of the pot needs to be addressed early on, and followed through in the finishing details. Handles can serve both a func-

tional and visual purpose on very large platters. Of course, they make it easier to carry, but they also provide an area where you can exercise your design sense. As shown here, thrown handles echo the construction of the platter, and can visually continue a line started in the rim.

Throwing the Platter

To get started, you'll need 10 pounds of clay and an 18 inch bat, a fettling knife, rubber rib, metal trimming tool, needle tool, a sponge and chamois, a kitchen scouring pad and a Surform tool.

Center and open up the ball of clay, leaving about ½ inch-thick base in the center (figure 1). If you are not used to throwing large pieces of clay, make sure that the clay you're using is a little softer than normal, and slow the wheel down slightly as you

114

1 Center and open the clay, leaving the base ½ inch thick.

2 Create a base that is 17 inches in diameter.

3 Smooth and compress the base using a rubber rib.

4 Create the rim shape in the thickened upper wall section.

center. Use both hands if necessary to create the center opening: overlap your hands, and use the upper hand to reinforce the pressure of the fingers that are in contact with the clay as you create the center hole. This will steady your hands and help with the added resistance of a large piece of clay.

Slow the wheel down slightly. Pull (or push) out the clay so that the base of the platter is about 17 inches in diameter (figure 2).

Using the palm of your hand, smooth the clay out evenly. This will condense and strengthen the base at the same time.

Use a rubber kidney to finish com-pressing the bottom, smooth out the throwing lines and giving a slight rounding of the base as it meets the wall (figure 3).

Starting where the base meets the wall, thin and pull up the wall about halfway. Take care not to thin this bottom wall section too much, or it won't be able to support the thickened rim. By stopping halfway, you've given yourself a lot of clay at the top to create a distinctive rim shape.

With your fingers supporting the outside of the rim, press down with your thumbs on the top of the clay to define the rim (figure 4). Keep your thumbs tightly together. Repeat this

Create an undercut using a fettling knife.

Throw an open bottom cylinder for the handles.

Use your fingers to create ridges that match the rim.

Trim the leather-hard platter using a Surform.

until you are happy with your rim, then go back and pull up the half-thrown wall to its full height. When you're finished throwing, the walls should be about ¼ inch, and the piece should be about 3 inches high.

Always check your base thickness when you finish throwing. It should be at least a quarter of an inch at the side and a little thicker in the center. Your cutting wire will tend to lift slightly at the center and the slightly thicker bottom allows for this. About an hour after throwing, trim off excess clay from the outside edge of the base with a pointed

wooden knife tool and use a fettling knife to undercut the pot about a ½ inch in from the edge to help facilitate your cutting wire (figure 5). I do this on any pot I intend to trim later. Since the pot is still attached to the bat, and therefore centered, the indented ring made by the knife on the bottom of the pot is accurate to the center of the pot while the clay edges are often not. This ring will also help you center your pot for trimming.

Cut about an hour after throwing, keeping the wire pressed down on the bat as you run it under the base. After running the wire under

9 Cut out handle shapes, and balls of clay for reinforcement.

10 Trim excess clay from the bottom of the handle.

11 Attach balls of clay to the ends of the handles and the rim.

12 Smooth the handle and rim with a chamois.

the piece once, rotate the bat ¼ turn and run the wire under again.

Throwing the Handles

After you've finished throwing the platter, set it aside to dry and create the handles. The handles designed for this platter come from a thrown ring and attach to the top of the rim. Center a 1 pound ball of and create a center hole that is open through to the bat. Pull the open doughnut of clay out to a diameter that leaves enough clay to form an upright ring about 1½ high (the width of your pot rim) (figure 6). Supporting the inner wall and the rim with one hand, use two fingers to push into the outside wall to form a shape with similar ridges as your pot rim (figure 7). Cut into the outside of the circle with a fettling knife and repeat on the inside taking care not to cut all the way through which could distort the thin walls.

Assembling the Pot

When the platter is leather hard, center it upside down on the wheel and use a Surform tool to flatten and trim the bottom and sides of the platter (figure 8).

Use a steel kidney to smooth the bottom and sides. Finally, cut a 45°

deckle or bevel on the edge. This gives a precise mark for where to start cleaning the underside after glazing and, on the completed piece, creates a shadow that gives the platter a slight visual lift.

When it's leather hard, cut a suitable length for each handle from the thrown ring, slicing it vertically down to the bat. Then, make eight balls of clay, each a little larger than a marble for reinforcing the attachment between the handle and the rim (figure 9).

Use a sharp knife to trim the sides of the handle that were attached to the bat (figure 10). This will roughly resemble the thrown top.

Using a damp scouring pad (Scotchbrite), roughly smooth the cut edges. Finish off with a sponge.

Divide the platter in half visually and make a small mark on opposite sides of the rim. Take the crescent shaped handles, dampen the edges and gently work them backwards to form flattened out areas to attach to the platter. On each side of your marked edge, score the rim and apply slip. Place the handle in position over the slip and push down and along the joint attaching the handle to the platter. Dip one ball of clay in water or slip (I use a little vinegar in either because it helps clay adhesion) and place it at the base of the handle. Supporting the underside of the rim, press down and along, attaching the ball to the handle and rim (figure 11). Repeat the process with the remaining balls of clay, using four for each handle. In addition to reinforcing the join, the added clay provides a visual transition between the handle and rim. Clean up the handles and rim using a wet chamois or piece of leather (figure 12).

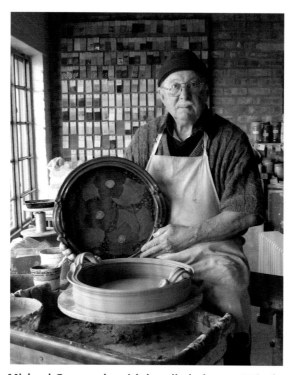

Michael Guassardo with handled platter, 17 inches in diameter, light colored fine grog stoneware with a transparent base glaze layered with cobalt, copper red, transparent blue, chrome green and rutile glazes, fired to cone 12 in reduction.

Lana Wilson's
Textured Platter

by Annie Chrietzberg

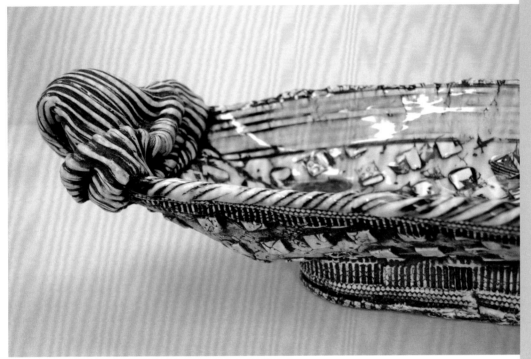

Detail of one of Lana Wilson's richly textured platters.

Lana Wilson's career spans more than 40 years and includes a vast repertoire of pieces and surface considerations, which she regularly shares with students. She teaches, on average, a workshop a month, and loves to do so. "It's so easy, really. The people are always interesting; you are instantly submerged in a milieu of like-minded people. I love the humor, and people are so kind."

What Lana really appreciates about teaching workshops is how much diverse experience there is in the audience. "At any given time, your audience might include a nurse,

a kiln builder or a cook, and when people open up about those things, I learn so much," she said. "And, if I come across something in ceramics that I don't know about, I'll ask the audience, and more times than not, I'll learn the answer."

Lana worked with functional stoneware for the first seventeen years of her life in ceramics. And then, a job at a community college caught her eye, so, at age 43, she went back to school to get her master's degree. For Lana, graduate school completely changed the course of her work. "Number one, it opened up the way to lots of exploring and experiment-

1 Smooth out a slab, layer, and press in objects then texture the surface.

2 Use hand tools, stamps, and found objects to embellish the slab.

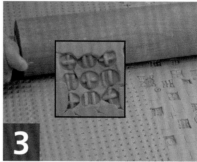

3 Roll over the texture with a rolling pin, to soften and tuck in the marks.

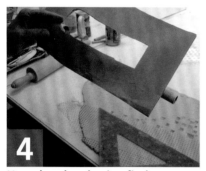

4 Use a handmade viewfinder to select an interesting area.

5 Cut out a dart then use it as a pattern to cut the remaining darts.

6 Lift and connect the edges where the darts have been removed.

ing, which has never ended," she said. "Number two, I started making non-functional work and using the electric kiln exclusively, neither of which I'd ever done before." Now, Lana's focus has returned to functional pieces. She told me one reason: "I want my grandchildren to eat off of things that I have made."

Texture Throughout

Lana applies texture in layers, and does so throughout her making process. During my visit, she made a serving platter to demonstrate how she works.

After using a slab roller to make a large slab, she lays out some fruit netting on the table, and sets the slab on top of it. This netting forms the basis of the texture composition on the back of the piece, though Lana will embellish it more at later stages. After smoothing the front of the slab with a small squeegee, Lana uses a wooden rolling pin from a pastry store to lay down some waffle texture, which created impressed squares, then in an adjacent area, she lay down and rolled over plastic sink mats that left larger, high-relief squares (figure 1). I watched her then target and go after some of the high relief squares with her small hand-held stamps, and some found objects, inverting them with embellishment (figure 2).

7 Prop the piece up, level the sides, and adjust as needed.

8 For handles, shape cones from large triangles cut from a textured slab.

9 Lift and drop the cone two or three times to get an organic shape.

10 Slip and score the handle in place, then support it with foam.

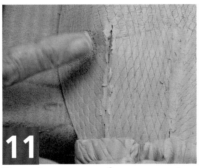

11 Turn piece over on foam supports, fill seams and adorn the repair.

12 Make a foot from a long, thin piece cut from a textured slab.

I was surprised when she picked up her rolling pin and rolled over the work she had just done (figure 3), but she explained to me, "You see, this softens it and makes it more interesting. I don't want it to look like plastic surgery. I don't like the whole Southern California glitzy sequin scene, I like old, worn friends. I like layers; I walk regularly in the Torrey Pines State Reserve when I'm home in San Diego. I love those layers of information around me."

I looked, and the effect she had created by rolling over existing texture was to 'tuck in' all the little marks she had made, like treasures in lockets. After tucking in her preliminary and secondary texture with a rolling pin, Lana embellished further with one of her new favorite items, the red scrubby applicator from a Shout bottle, and an old favorite, a seamstress' marking tool.

Forming the Platter

Lana had created a slab much larger than what she actually needed for the piece she had in mind. She cut a framing device out of a piece of paper roughly the proportions of her intended serving dish (figure 4). She used this viewfinder to locate the best part of her texture drawing, marked the boundaries by laying down a straight edge then, using the straight edge again, cut out the shape.

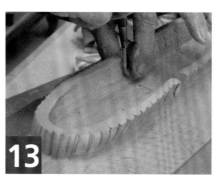

Smooth the foot with a roller and cut decorative arches through it.

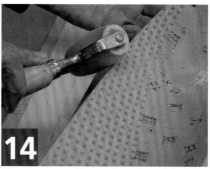

Use a pony roller to bevel and finish both sides of the platter's edge.

Lana needed to take two darts out of each end to have the flat shape rise up into the form she wanted. "Oh, I suppose I should use a template, but I never do," she quipped, knowing that I am a template fiend. "I can never find the one I need when I need it, besides, I know what shape I need to cut out, and after I cut the first one, I'll use it to cut the other three," she explained, as she cut out and removed the first dart.

She took the triangular piece of clay she removed, turned it over, and set it gently down to trace it where she wanted the second dart. She then took those two cut-out and placed them on the other end, and traced and cut out the remaining two darts (figure 5). The size of the dart determines the shape of the final form. After slipping and scoring, she simply lifted and butted the joining edges together (figure 6), and then used small pieces of foam to prop up the ends of the serving dish which allows them to firm up while sup-

ported. She fills in gaps in the texture where the darts were removed with paper clay to prevent cracks from forming along the seam.

To address the sides, Lana grabbed a couple of paint stirring sticks, which she used to lift the sides and then shoved pieces of foam beneath to hold them in place. She filled in gaps that had been made by cutting through existing texture on the edges, and then compressed and beveled those edges with a pony roller. Then, she used a spirit level to make sure the edges, were, um, level (figure 7). "I don't know a gallery who would take a piece that's not level," she murmured as she made slight adjustments. "There we go!"

Making Handles

The next task was to make the handles. First, she textures a slab and cuts out large triangles, then she rolls them into a cone (figure 8), seals them using a pony roller, and drops them on her workbench (figure 9).

They magically gain character with each whump. Once she is satisfied with the result, she cuts away excess clay with a fettling knife, scores and slips the end of the serving dish, as well as the inside of a handle, and then attaches it, stacking foam beneath it for support (figure 10).

Lana constantly manipulates the surface of her pieces as she is making, adding texture as she goes. After attaching the handles, she grabbed a wooden dowel with sharpened ends (a pencil would work, too) to both re-draw and enhance existing lines. After the piece had dried to leather hard, she removed the bolsters and turned it over on a large piece of foam to access the bottom. She filled the gaps in the seams with paper clay, again to strengthen them and prevent cracking (figure 11). When she makes a repair like this, she adorns it. "I could teach a whole course on cheating," she joked, while rolling a seamstress' marking tool over the filled-in seam.

Adding a Foot

The last part of the serving dish project was to make and attach a foot. Before she had turned the piece over, she had taken an approximate measurement with a seamstress' measuring tape, and had created a long slab to texture. She played around a bit with some scrap clay to determine the appropriate height, textured the slab, and used a straight edge to cut a long strip of clay for the foot. She picked up the long strip in loose folds and dropped it a few times on the table. "This makes an undulating line I just love," she told me as she worked.

She placed the foot on the bottom of the pot, shaped it how she wanted it, and cut the excess away, then joined the foot into a ring. After scoring and slipping the areas that need to be joined, she attached the foot ring to the bottom of the serving dish and used a dry soft brush to remove excess slip and blend the seam (figure 12). She then used a common loop tool to create a little looped arch on each side of the foot (figure 13). She rolled the edge with a pony roller, used a ware board to flip the piece right side up, and used the spirit level again to make adjustments (figure 14).

Lana has a delightfully free, direct, and easy way of making, but don't let that fool you into thinking she doesn't take her time in the studio seriously. "I've changed my style of work about six times through out my career., and each time it takes me about six months to a year to figure it out," she told me. "People don't realize that being an artist is really about daily discipline; when I'm working, I want my time to work. I'm not one of those ladies who does lunch. Ceramics is far too expansive for that."

Finishing

Lana Wilson's work is mostly black and white with bits of vibrant color splashed about. She says, "I have a background in painting, and this technique really appeals to the painter in me." She gleaned this current surface treatment from two artists, Denise Smith of Ann Arbor, Michigan, and Claudia Reese, a potter from Texas.

Simple Slip

To prepare the slip, Lana takes 100 grams of small pieces of bone dry clay and adds 10–50 grams of a stain. The percentages of stains varies according to the intensity of color she is trying to achieve.

The clay Lana uses is Half & Half from Laguna, formulated for firing at cone 5, though she fires it to cone 6. This clay body is half porcelain and half white stoneware. It's not as white as porcelain, but it does fire white rather than yellow in oxidation, isn't as finicky as porcelain, and works well with Lana's making methods. If you're buying clay from the East Coast, she suggests a clay body called Little Loafers from Highwater Clays.

Easy Application

The technique is simple. On a piece of bisqueware, first brush on black slip or one of the base colors (figure

CAUTION

You must wear a respirator during this stage. In the final step, she dips the piece in a clear glaze, and fires to cone 6. Through lots of experimenting, and with lots more to go, Lana finds that ending with a dark color on top works best for her.

NOTE

Stain-bearing slips applied to surfaces that come into contact with food need to be covered with a food-safe clear glaze.

1) then sponge it off, leaving slip in the crevices (figure 2). Then, using colored slips dab on bits of color here and there (figure 3). Remove some of that with steel wool (figure 4). "I can't use water for this step or it will muddy the colors," Lana explains.

Recipes

There are two groups of colored slips. The first group Lana uses for the base coat that she washes off, leaving color in all the recesses. The accent slips are more intense and removed with steel wool. All stains are Mason stains except for 27496 Persimmon Red, which is from Cerdec. Add the stains and bone dry clay to water and allow to sit for 30–60 minutes so it will mix easier.

Recipes

Base Coat or Wash Colors

6600 Best Black	10%
6339 Royal Blue	5-10 %
6069 Dark Coral	35%

Accent Slips

6129 Golden Ambrosia	30%
6485 Titanium Yellow	20%
6024 Orange	30%
6236 Chartreuse	50%
6027 Tangerine	15%
6211 Pea Green	50%
6288 Turquoise	50%
6242 Bermuda	10%
6069 Dark Coral	35%
6122 Cedar	25%
6304 Violet	60%
K5997 Cherry Red*	30%
27496 Persimmon Red (Cerdec)*	30%

* inclusion pigments

Kate the Younger Clear Glaze

Cone 6

Ferro Frit 3195	70 %
EPK Kaolin	8
Wollastonite	10
Silica	12
	100 %
Add: Bentonite	2 %

From Richard Burkett. Use over colored slips. Shiny, resistant to crazing, cool slowly.

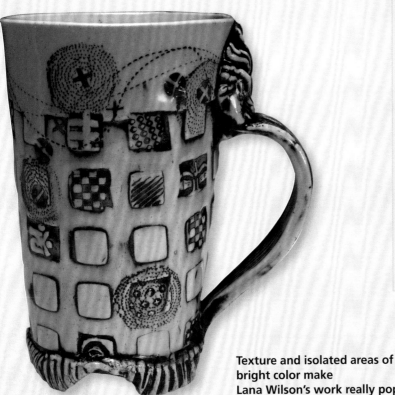

Texture and isolated areas of bright color make Lana Wilson's work really pop.

Thrown Square Baker

by Dick Lehman

Thrown square baking dish, 12 in. (30 cm) in width, stoneware, fired to cone 10 reduction.

Several decades ago, I attended an NCECA conference in San Antonio. I was only a few years into my life as a full-time potter and was especially keen to see a demonstration by John Glick, the 'godfather of American studio ceramics' and one of my heroes. As the "Roger Bannister" of potters, he broke the four-minute mile for studio potters, showing that it was possible to be a self-sustaining studio potter while pursuing a life's dream. Now I finally had the opportunity to see him work first-hand!

Although I only remember a few aspects of John's presentation, I do specifically remember that John used a wooden template to create a beaded foot on some large flat bowls. After he established the foot, he cut and overlapped the rim of the bowl, a design recognized as vintage Glick. Then—and this is the important part—he used that wooden template to "draw" a series of backward "C's" into the foot of the pot as the pot slowly turned. The result was a kind of lobed foot that mimicked the wave action of the bowl's rim.

Fast forward a couple of decades and I'm in my studio working on some new low baking dish forms. I decided to try Glick's footing method using my own wooden template, hoping to discover something about the process that I could use—something of integrity that was tied to my own aesthetic and not just a mimicking of his design.

Here, of course, is where the genius of individual temperament and

Begin by throwing a low, wide, straight-sided cylinder.

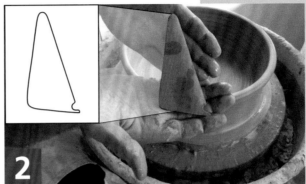

Profile of the wooden rib used to create the beaded foot and square off the pot.

With the wheel spinning, create the beaded foot, press the rib against the outside of the form at a 45° angle.

Add design lines to the rim. These will be accentuated later by the alterations to the shape.

neurological wiring take over. My natural inclination toward "lysdexia" (dyslexia) kicked in, and instead of carving backward C's into the foot with the wooden rib, I began unconsciously carving big looping forward-facing C's! So instead of a lotus-like lobing of the foot, my pot suddenly became a beautiful six-sided baking dish. I could hardly believe the fortuitous consequence of my dyslexia!

From this discovery, I quickly moved to making three-sided, squared, rectangular, five-sided and oval forms. I made taller jars and vases, large serving bowls and bottles, and before long, a handled, dancing diamond-shaped baking dish, the body of which is made from one piece of clay.

Throwing the Form

To create a diamond-shaped baking dish, begin by throwing a low, straight-sided cylinder (figure 1). I used about four pounds of clay for the piece shown in this demonstration. Next, with the wheel spinning, create a beaded foot by pressing a notched wooden rib (figure 2) against the outside of the cylinder at a 45° angle (figure 3). I usually choose to

5 Designate the four corner areas, then begin squaring the form by pressing the rib into the four sides. Release pressure as you approach the corners.

6 Change the shape of the pot gradually, over the course of 10 to12 revolutions of the wheel.

7 Using one finger, pull the corners gently outward to accentuate the square shape.

8 Articulate the foot by pressing in at intervals to create a "dancing square" shape.

Detail of an undulating squared-off baker made directly on the wheel.

add some design lines to the rim so that the later alteration becomes more pronounced due to the repeated lines and shadows (figure 4).

For the rib, you can make your own by using a file to create a contour of your own design in the edge of a plain wooden rib. The rib shown in the photos is one that I made from three thin sheets of osage orange glued together with the grain of the wood alternating at 90° angles. After cutting out the contour of the rib, I sanded the edges smooth. (Note: Maple, beech or any fruit wood (apple, pear, cherry) are suitable woods to use for making pottery tools.)

Altering the Form

To begin squaring the form, designate the four corners. I often put marks on the bat or place little balls of clay on the wheel head to mark these corners. Next, with the wheel rotating very slowly, begin gently pushing the wooden template into the four sides between the marks, releasing pressure when you get to the corners (figure 5). The shape does not change abruptly so the pot may revolve ten or twelve times until you achieve a fairly square profile (figure 6). You may notice that where the wall has been pushed inward, little

9 Manipulate the rim to mimic the articulation and lines of the beaded foot.

10 Pull, extrude or roll out two small lug handles and attach them while the pot is still on the wheel.

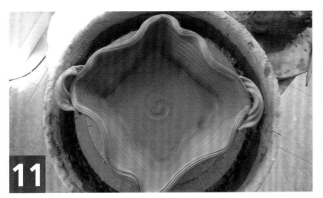

11 Top view showing the undulating shape of the pot.

12 Detail showing the articulation and indentations made to the outside of the pot during the squaring process.

"wrinkles" will form on the inside corners where the inside wall meets the bottom of the pot. This is not a problem and a gentle sponging will smooth those wrinkles.

To accentuate the sense of square-ness, gently pull the corners outward with one finger (figure 7). If you simply want a square pot, you could stop at this point. I usually continue by articulating the foot— pushing it even farther with the wooden rib, creating a kind of "dancing square" shape (figure 8). Then I manipulate the rim to mimic the foot's articulation and line (figure 9).

Finishing Touches

For a dish to be used in the oven, I attach handles while the pot is still wet on the wheel (figure 10). These handles can be pulled from a lump of clay, made from rolled coils or slabs, or extruded. The finished form (figure 11) reveals the shape of this dancing-square pot, and a detail image of the articulation I added to the exterior of the foot (figure 12). This method works equally well for making rect-angular and oval forms. Taller forms can be altered by the same method to create, for example, square vases.

Abstract Reflection

by Lauren Sandler

Bowl forms are particularly interesting for decorating because they provide an expansive landscape to explore. A generous open object when functioning, a bowl acts as an offering yet also as an object of containment—a reservoir of reverie and reflection. It's this paradox of offering and containment that I find most alluring and attempt to expand upon with my surface work.

Making the Mold

Begin by making a clay mold that will be used to drape a slab over. The mold will be used to make the bottom quarter of the final bowl form that will then be built up to the finished shape and height with coils. The mold is made upside down and solid—later it will be turned upright and hollowed out. I start by drawing a boundary line to follow by first cutting out a paper pattern for what will be the top of the mold (when upright) and outlining that on the bat (figure 1). I begin the mold with a large thick slab, cut around the drawn line then add and remove clay as needed to create the desired form (figure 2). Take your time in shaping the mold; even out and smooth the surface with a Surform tool or rasp, then refine the shape and the surface with metal and rubber ribs. Place a bat and a torpedo level on top of the form and make any adjustments needed until it is level (figure 3).

Once the mold has set up to a firm leather hard (wet enough to hollow out, but firm enough to hold its shape when handled) turn it upright and examine it. Check the shape to assure that the shape is what you're looking for and add or remove clay as needed. At this point you can hollow out the form leaving ½-inch thick walls (figure 4). Once finished, let the mold dry for a few days. The mold doesn't have to be bone dry before using—just dry enough so the slab won't stick to it.

For a longer lasting mold, you may want to make a plaster one; although I have been using some of the same bone-dry clay molds for a couple of years—that includes many moves. The edges will often chip, but I usually cut the bottom part of the slab off above the chipped parts so it doesn't interfere with the form.

Using the Mold

Roll out a ⅛–¼-inch thick slab that's large enough to drape over the mold (figure 5). I usually make a slab large enough to get two to three pieces out of it. Don't let the slab get too dry before using it or it will crack when draped over the mold. I prefer my slabs on the wet side—just dry enough so they won't stick to the mold—I let them do most of their drying on the mold. Place the slab over the mold and shape it to the mold. Once the slab has stiffened enough to hold its shape, cut off the

excess clay from the bottom using an X-Acto knife (figure 6).

Swiftly lift the slab up, loosening it from all four corners and stand it upright. Even the rim using a Surform and bevel the inside of the rim to prepare it for a coil (figure 7). Check the level of the pot again here. You may have to gently tap the pot on its foot to make sure it's level. Wrap the rim with a damp paper towel and plastic to prepare for adding coils. Leave the bottom unwrapped to stiffen in order to support the weight of added coils.

Because of the setting up time needed in coil building, I work on many pieces at once, putting another slab on the mold right after I take one off. I can build this form in one day, but time varies depending on the size and complexity.

Preparing and Adding Coils

Roll out a large coil the length of the circumference of the pot's rim. I use a thread to measure the rim and coil. Slightly flatten the coil with your hand and bevel the edge that attaches to the interior beveled edge of the pot with your hand or small rolling pin. Add the coil, overlap the ends a bit and cut through both. Bevel both ends and attach (figure 8). You don't need to slip and score since the clay is wet enough to be blended together easily. Blend the coil to the interior of the pot first, then Surform the exterior where the coil and the wall meet to smooth it out and add and blend a small coil around the exterior (fig-

Using a paper pattern, trace the outline of the top of the mold.

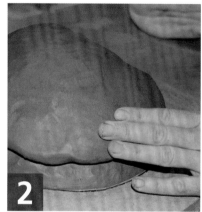

Add clay to the mold, taking care to remain inside your outline.

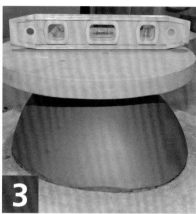

Smooth the surface, then level the bottom of the mold.

Hollow out the leather-hard mold, leaving ½-inch thick walls.

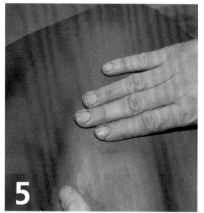

Drape a soft slab over the mold, completely covering it.

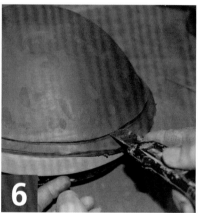

Fit the slab to the mold, then trim excess clay with an X-Acto knife.

ure 9). Repeat these steps until you get the desired size.

Finishing the Rim

Once you have the desired height and volume, even out the rim with a Surform, then measure and mark the four corners of the rim using a string and ruler. Decide how much of a curve you would like and mark the lowest point on two opposite sides of the rim. Use the Surform to cut the clay away moving from one side to the other (figure 10) to main-

tain the same amount of pressure. Once you have the curve defined, smooth the rim using your fingers or a rib. (figure 11).

Finishing the Pot

My current surface work comes from the desire to use my pots as a space to abstractly render elements of my life, observations, and reflections. I'm interested in breaking up the surface of the form and creating spaces within and upon the object. The division of space through line

7 Bevel interior edge to prepare it for an added coil.

8 Add a large, slightly flattened coil to the rim and blend the interior seam.

9 Add a thin coil to outside wall where the larger coil and the pot meet.

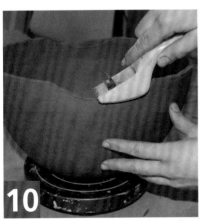

10 Remove clay down to marks and create a gradual curve to the rim.

11 Smooth out and finish the curve and soften the rim.

12 Apply the base coat of terra sigillata using a soft brush.

and color provide symbolic opportunities to explore paradoxical states of interior and exterior, expansiveness and constriction, possibility and unattainability, connections and missconnections. Essentially the surface of a pot is a place where the inward and the outward meet, a means of finding connections through our shared interior worlds.

I prefer terra sigillata to glaze for its soft and non-reflective surface. I want to keep the surface in a raw state—as close as possible in appearance to unfired clay—that's when the clay is most vibrant and most resembles skin and our bodies.

Before brushing on the sigillata I decide the design and general layout of the surface, how it will be divided, what colors I will use, where I want the red glaze to be, and how I want the dots and drips of red glaze to connect or disconnect. Although I make a lot of decisions as I am working, I do think about the relationship of the red dots and the corresponding line work, that being the central

13 Apply final layers of terra sig, incise lines, add glaze details.

133

Recipes

Cushing's White Terra Sigillata

Water	14	cups
OM4 Ball Clay	1500	grams
Deflocculant	0.1-0.3	%

Colors: In same sequence of the cups. All oxide/stain measurements are with one cup of terra sigillata

Yellow

Mason Stain 6464 Zirconium Yellow	½ tsp

Red

Red Iron Oxide	½ tsp

Blue/Green

Mason Stain 6464 Zirconium Yellow	½ tsp
Mason Stain 6305 Teal Blue	½ tsp

White

Titanium dioxide	1 tsp
Chrome Green	
Chrome oxide	⅛ tsp

I don't use a ball mill when making terra sig. I mix up the batch, let it sit for a few days than siphon off the top layer of water then I siphon off the sigillata and put it in a glass container. When I use it, I mix one cup sigillata with the specific oxides. Be sure to wear gloves and a mask when handling oxides and stains.

I add about ½ to 1 teaspoon of gerstley borate to each cup of sigillata to lower the flux rate. I find this helps with sealing the surface. It may affect the smoothness of the fired surface, in which case I use a 220-grit sandpaper over the pots after firing.

Red Glaze: Unfortunately I recently found out that the red glaze I have been using is no longer being made. I have yet to start using another – still watering down the bits of dried red glaze left, but in the past I've used Duncan 1206-Neon Red.

Clear Glaze: Spectrum 700 Clear

Clay: Archie Bray Foundation Earthenware

part of the surface design, and that which the rest revolves around. I will consider the condition and position of the red dots – is there a tension between them? How will the lines move over the form? Will they connect on one side and disconnect on another? Will it be an isolated dot? Or a cluster?

I view the different sides of a form as passages of time, or spaces of transition, using color and line to establish the division or movement. Often a line may move in various directions throughout the surface, having to navigate in and around the different blocks of color. The change of color with incised lines along the borders conveys a shift between interior and exterior, creating channels for lines and dots to move through, come out of, or reside in.

My color choices vary, sometimes it is more of an aesthetic decision, which color is most pleasing or intriguing with the other, and other times it is based on contrast and I think more in terms of light and dark to make clear distinctions of surface

Once I decide the general layout, I begin by applying the base coat. I wait until the clay is bone dry before applying the sigillata—if done earlier, the clay won't absorb the sigillata and it will take a long time in between coats to dry. I use a hake brush because it holds a lot of liquid, moves well on the surface and doesn't leave brush marks (figure 12). I apply two to four coats of sigil-

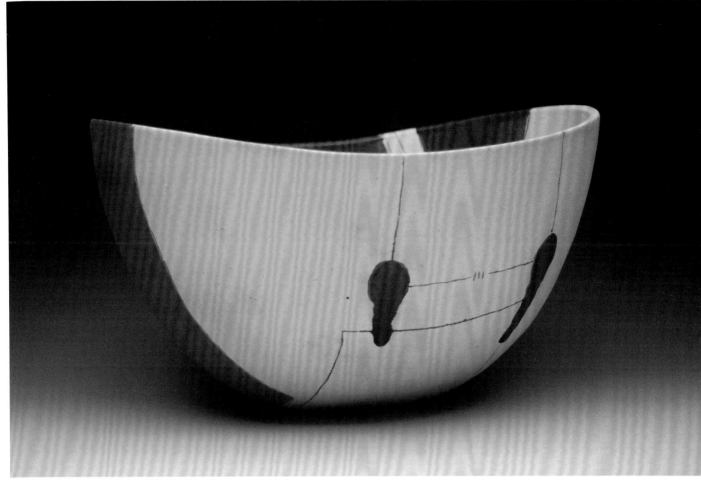

The finished earthenware bowl, fired to cone 03.

lata, depending on thickness; if it is too thick, the sigillata will peel off the fired surface. Let each coat dry before applying the next. After the final coat (of base color), but before the sigillata has completely dried—darker in color, cold to the touch, but not leaving any finger marks on the surface, I rub it using a small piece of foam until I get a shine to the surface. I prefer foam to plastic because it moves more easily across the surface.

The second color is brushed over the first, I start by using a thin brush to paint the outline then I fill in the spaces with a wider brush, usually two light coats and taking care not to apply it too thick, in order to avoid it chipping off after firing. This is followed by the incised line work using a pin tool and the application of the red glaze (figure 13). A clear glaze is applied to the interior of the pot after the bisque firing then fired to cone 03.

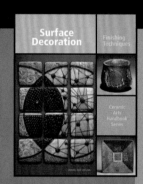

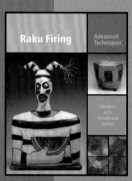

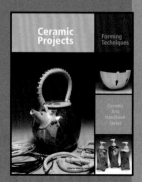